APPLYING CRITICAL THINKING AND ANALYSIS IN SOCIAL WORK

MICHAELA ROGERS ☒
DAN ALLEN ☒

Los Angeles | London | New Delhi
Singapore | Washington DC | Melbourne

Los Angeles | London | New Delhi
Singapore | Washington DC | Melbourne

SAGE Publications Ltd
1 Oliver's Yard
55 City Road
London EC1Y 1SP

SAGE Publications Inc.
2455 Teller Road
Thousand Oaks, California 91320

SAGE Publications India Pvt Ltd
B 1/I 1 Mohan Cooperative Industrial Area
Mathura Road
New Delhi 110 044

SAGE Publications Asia-Pacific Pte Ltd
3 Church Street
#10-04 Samsung Hub
Singapore 049483

Editor: Kate Keers
Assistant editor: Talulah Hall
Production editor: Martin Fox
Copyeditor: Richard Leigh
Proofreader: Sharon Cawood
Marketing manager: Samantha Glorioso
Cover design: Wendy Scott
Typeset by: C&M Digitals (P) Ltd, Chennai, India
Printed and bound by CPI Group (UK) Ltd, Croydon
CR0 4YY

Library of Congress Control Number: 2018960246

British Library Cataloguing in Publication data

A catalogue record for this book is available from the British Library

ISBN 978-1-5264-3657-3
ISBN 978-1-5264-3658-0 (pbk)

CONTENTS

ABOUT THE AUTHORS

Dr Michaela Rogers is a Senior Lecturer in Social Work at the University of Sheffield. Dr Rogers is involved in both research and teaching across the areas of social care, social justice, equality and diversity, safeguarding, interpersonal violence and gender. She has worked alongside colleagues on a range of projects in the voluntary and public sectors. These projects typically aim to explore social problems in terms of everyday experiences or assess the impact of service delivery or specific policy initiatives. Dr Rogers is a qualified social worker registered with the profession's regulatory body in England, the Health and Care Professions Council.

Dr Dan Allen is the Head of Stakeholder Engagement and Research at the Disclosure and Barring Service (DBS). A former social work practitioner and academic, with over 16 years' experience working to democratise child protection practice with Romani and Traveller families, he now uses his research and practice experience to design and implement a best-in-class stakeholder engagement and research function that informs government strategy and policy. Dr Allen is a qualified social worker registered with the profession's regulatory body in England, the Health and Care Professions Council.

INTRODUCTION

In this book, we will establish the fact that critical thinking is a fundamental social work skill. Like any skill, though, critical thinking requires practice. In a similar way to Serena and Venus Williams practising for hours on the tennis courts to become world-beating athletes, you need to practise your skill of critical thinking to become a proud, safe, effective and capable social worker. It is unlikely that your hard work will be rewarded with the same fame and fortune that Serena and Venus enjoy, but, by taking the time to develop your critical thinking skills, you will be setting yourself on a pathway to achieve the best social work practice possible – and what better reward could there be than that?

The importance of critical thinking

Aiming to become the best social work practitioner possible requires you to understand that the people whom you work to support will most likely remember you for a long time. Your involvement in people's lives will be memorable. What is crucially important, therefore, is that you work hard to ensure that the memories that people will have of you are positive. It might be that some people disagree that they need social work involvement in their lives; others might not share your views and assessment of a particular situation. Nevertheless, by promoting opportunities for effective relationships, and by working in a safe, open and transparent way, you should be able to use critical reflection to justify your actions and explain why some of the decisions you make in partnership with the people you are working with are right.

Critical reflection is a skill that varies from person to person and from one social worker to another. It is an essential characteristic of social work practice because even with the best intentions, social work practitioners can make mistakes. The key difference between safe, effective and capable social work practice and social work practice that falls short of the required minimum standards is the ability to apply critical reflection skills well. As you will uncover throughout this book, the single biggest factor undermining the skills required to critically reflect well is you. Critical reflection and critical writing require that we turn a mirror onto our own practice to see and examine our actions and writing in the most objective way possible.

By the end of your social work training, you will have worked to support people who will almost certainly remember you for the rest of their lives. For some of you this reality might be unnerving; after all, the privilege of being so heavily involved in the lives of others is a challenge that you might not have fully considered or understood at the outset of this learning journey. But the point to try to always remember is that if you work as hard as you can to ensure that the memories people have of you reflect the diligence of your work, rather than any of the omissions that you might make, you will be progressing along the right path.

In *Social Work as Art* by Hugh England (1986), social work is conceptualised as a process by which you, through the intuitive use of self, give meaning to the lived experiences of others. As you engage with the world around you, it is arguable that you are now skilled, as a mature learner, to use all of your senses to understand and develop a strong notion of what type of relationships you like with others and what type of relationships you do not like. In other words, you have developed the social skills needed to develop and maintain or distance yourself from various relationships that you have with others. Throughout your own life course development, you have been taught, and have learnt, how to interact with others, how to communicate and how to be successful in achieving your own ambitions.

In the body of England's (1986) writing, social work is seen to operate from an individual's use of intuition which has been learnt over their lifetime. Almost as a predictive reaction against the increasingly dominant scientific and evaluative crisis-driven models of intervention that social work has seemingly sleepwalked into, his work requires you to apply the use of self as the single most important measure in any social work activity. For him, the 'art' of practice is found within you and should be shared by you with all others less fortunate than yourself. What this means in practice is that the difference between good practice and bad practice is you, the difference between a good assessment and a bad assessment is you, the difference between effective relationships and negative relationships is you.

Omissions are a part of your learning journey. As with most experiences, trying something new often necessitates learning from mistakes. If you were learning to make a chocolate cake, for instance, you might imagine several failed attempts before mastering the recipe (and use of the oven). There is a world of difference between baking a chocolate cake and doing social work practice, however, because of the inescapable fact that if you make a mistake with another person, you cannot easily start over again, particularly as you might be heavily involved in that person's life. While you learn, you must ensure that you fully acknowledge and fully address any implications of your actions. You should do this because you work with people, and understand that when working with people you are working from a position of power.

At a fundamental level, one might assume that England's (1986) thesis suggests that the 'art' of practice can be mastered if you provide the same service to others as you yourself might expect to receive. While this value position might be valid as a foundation, it is important to critically consider and respect the fact that the needs of others do not always reflect your own preferences, desires or intentions. This is not to suggest that England (1986) is wrong, but it does imply the need to problematise his principle of 'intuitive' social work. On this basis, you would do well to consider how your own learnt intuitions (such as values, knowledge, skills, attitudes, communication styles and prejudices) might have culminated to make you an effective adult, but might not make you an effective social worker.

In contemporary social work, working at the interface of chronic socio-economic injustice, reductions in public spending and the yawning gap between the privileged and those oppressed by overt and covert systems of injustice, the 'art' of practice advanced in this book requires you to acknowledge your presuppositions, put them to one side and develop the professional skills needed to understand what life is like for the people you are working to support. Before you contemplate this reality in much more detail, remember that you were born with two ears and one mouth, to ensure that you listen twice as much as you speak (think about it ...). What this means for you is that you can only hope to understand the lived experiences of others if you suspend all judgement until such time as judgement is required. Learning when this occasion may be is undoubtedly problematical, and for this reason we see the application of judgement as the single most important aspect of professional intuition. This is one reason why the need to learn the 'art' of practice, in addition to whatever you might already feel you know, forms the key focus of this book.

Developing skills in critical thinking can be challenging as you are asked to turn a mirror onto yourself and onto your own practice. It requires you to look carefully at the way you do social work and to consider how other people perceive you as a social worker. To help guide you through this process, this book features many case studies, theoretical explainers, activities, questions and danger points. Used together, they have been designed to facilitate opportunities for you to become a critical thinker and move on into practice with the capabilities and confidence needed to be safe and effective. Indeed, we hope that you use this book as you seek to navigate each element of your learning journey in social work.

As you progress through this book, each chapter provides you with key information and practical opportunities which you might like to pursue in preparation for professional practice. As you complete the activities that are provided you are encouraged to record your reflections and keep them somewhere handy. These reflections will be useful as you read through and revisit the various chapters presented and they will enable you to begin to maintain a log of your learning. Recording your learning in this way might seem like a tedious activity, but be assured that the encouragement being given here will help your progression through this book, and the whole of your career.

Structure of the book

As an introductory text on critical thinking, we have designed this book to be appealing to those who wish to develop their practical skills as well as to those who wish to develop their theoretical skills. We start in Part I with a broad theoretical illustration of the position of critical thinking within social work. In Part II we will consider the more rudimentary and pragmatic elements of critical reading and critical writing. In Part III we will then explore the practical application of the skills described and the theories proposed, and each chapter will introduce you to those critical skills which you must have when entering education on pre-qualifying social work programmes.

Recognising that critical reflection is a skill that varies from person to person (there will be more on this later), we recognise that this might not be a book that you read from cover to cover. Instead, you might be more targeted in your reading and use the nine chapters of this book as and when you need them. As experienced social work practitioners and academics, we recognise that you might want to visit and revisit these chapters at different stages of your training and experience as an early career social worker, as your own practice wisdom becomes more defined.

Part I begins with a chapter that establishes the basis of critical thinking as the process by which social workers reflect on and interpret situations with thoughtful connections to other events or circumstances. Using examples from practice, this chapter will show how uncritical practice can lead to reactive judgements and misuses of power and position. It introduces the concept of critical thinking as a skill that can be practised and developed to mitigate uncritical value-based judgements. We will introduce key writers, such as Brookfield. We will highlight the theoretical and empirical knowledge base of critical thinking while engaging you in lots of practical activities to identify and develop a sense of their own confidence as critical thinkers. We will link the discussions and activities to the Professional Capabilities Framework to demonstrate the relevance of this skill in terms of social work practice. We will encourage you to consider the strengths, limitations and barriers to critical thinking in university and practice.

Chapter 2 builds on the concepts, tools and strategies developed in Chapter 1 to consider the core details of critical thinking in more practical detail. By establishing the basis of using theoretical and empirical knowledge to inform practice, rather than as something that might be associated with practice in hindsight, this chapter will begin to develop your awareness of the importance of working in a systematic and evidence-informed way. We will provide examples to illuminate the importance of substantiating decisions made in practice with theoretical and empirical knowledge so that a critical justification can be given for any actions that are taken or not.

After establishing the theoretical terms, concepts and models that underpin critical thinking and analysis, Part II will develop the requisite skills needed to embed critical thinking within the praxis of social work and education. Chapter 3 will commence this process by highlighting the importance of critical reading. We will introduce the different sources of knowledge, taking a critical stance to explore how these influence social work policy and practice. We will explore different types of knowledge (primary, secondary, tertiary), contrasting these with the notion of 'experts by experience' to problematise the application of knowledge in social work education and practice contexts. This will involve demonstrating a critical orientation towards the recommendations advanced by theoretical and empirical knowledge found within the social work literature. We will integrate examples from practice to illuminate the tensions and risks associated with uncritical value-based judgements. This chapter will illustrate the importance of critical reading as applied to different types of knowledge.

Chapter 4 will help you identify the differences between description and analysis within the academic assignment. As a foundation from which to grow and nurture the knowledge, values and skills needed to develop critical thinking, we will provide you with lots of examples of the writing techniques and tools required in student assignments and practical advice about how to develop and embed analysis within a piece of academic writing. These examples will guide you through the common mistakes made by students in critical writing and show, by example, how to improve written work through the critical application and substantiation of evidence in written assignments.

Part III focuses on the application of critical and analytical skills in social work practice. Chapter 5 explains why critical reflection forms the basis of practice learning and is an essential skill which students must demonstrate in order to progress in their social work education and professional training. We will introduce common models for reflective practice and problematise them in application. We will explore the task of reflective writing and, in doing so, will draw on the themes of the earlier chapters to demonstrate how these critical skills are essential in demonstrating competency and in the core function of social work (in the tasks of assessment and analysis).

Chapter 6 then considers professional judgement and decision-making, and suggests that the most common, problematic tendency in student reflection is the limited confidence to review judgements and plans once a view has been formed on what is going on. Students often struggle to notice or to dismiss evidence that challenges an initial impression. This chapter will provide you with a view of the techniques and strategies that can be used to ensure that decisions are being made upon verifiable fact, rather than unsubstantiated supposition. Problematising the notion of a 'gut reaction', this chapter will encourage you to critically reflect on and analyse evidence that challenges the notion of confirmation bias.

Chapter 7 presents a number of opportunities to improve professional practice but also highlights some limitations in the assumption that individual practice, organisation structures and socio-economic structures might not always support good and effective practice. Students can develop a sense of defeat as they focus on limitations rather than strengths. Positioning reflection as a tool to identify and develop professional practice, this chapter will help you develop the confidence to critically analyse and substantiate good practice. Ours is a profession which struggles to celebrate success, and this chapter will encourage you to consider your own practice through strengths-based perspectives so that you can come to see yourself, your learning and your role in promoting social justice and change in a more constructive and balanced way.

Chapter 8 builds on Chapter 5 to explain why the responsibility to reflect *before* action, *in* action and then *on* action is so central to social work practice. We will explain why effective, safe and competent practice requires a sensitive awareness of the views and perceptions of others. At this level, the social worker is constantly thinking about how social work practices are affecting the experiences of and outcomes for people being supported. The social worker's goal is to continually improve practice and outcomes for people and their communities. Highlighting opportunities and strategies to consider the use of self and reflexivity, this chapter will facilitate opportunities for you to critically consider how your own learnt values, knowledge, skills, attitudes, communication styles and prejudices affect your ability to assess and analyse the lives of others effectively and credibly.

The final Chapter 9 recognises why analytical assessments and report writing are core social work skills that require a significant commitment to continual professional development and self-awareness. Highlighting the central importance of evidence-based and evidence-informed practice that draws on the indigenous knowledge of the people social work seeks to support, this chapter will consider the assessment process. We will include some practical guidance on barriers to completing analytical assessment, while offering some tools and techniques to help you address issues of engagement, power, resistance and complexity. The chapter will then move on to offer a very practical guide to integrating analysis in report writing. We will offer tips, do's and don'ts, and examples of practice to help you to understand what analysis means in terms of written reports. There will be some discussion of the purpose of reports, engaging you in a discourse that serves to reflect on the statutory nature of the social work role.

The conclusion will provide a summary of the preceding nine chapters, reiterating that fact that critical reflection requires skill, patience and practice. Concluding the golden thread that runs throughout this book, this chapter will encourage you to critically consider why the difference between good critical reflection and unreflected action is you.

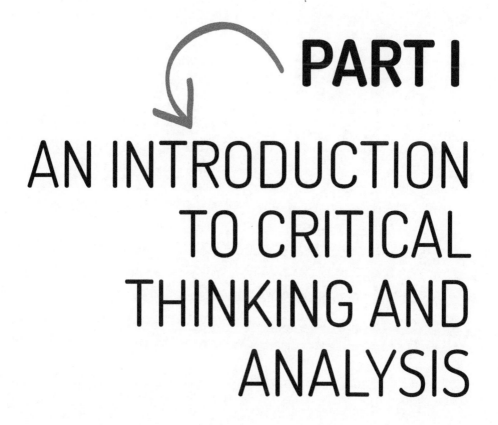

PART I

AN INTRODUCTION TO CRITICAL THINKING AND ANALYSIS

1

INTRODUCTION TO
CRITICAL THINKING

.... THEORETICAL BACKGROUND

- Critical thinking
- Bloom's taxonomy
- De Bono's Six Thinking Hats®

.... RELEVANCE TO SOCIAL WORK THINKING AND PRACTICE

- Applying knowledge to practice
- Anti-oppressive practice
- Practice wisdom
- Professional Capabilities Framework

.... REAL-WORLD CHALLENGES

- Pathologising and cultural relativist reactions
- Low confidence, insecurity and lack of familiarity

Introduction

As a practice-based profession and an academic discipline that promotes social change and development, social cohesion, and the empowerment and liberation of people (Veal et al., 2016), social work education places an ever-increasing emphasis on the need for social work students to be critical in their thinking (Fook and Askeland, 2007). Student social workers who can analyse information objectively and then make a reasoned judgement tend to progress through their studies, and professional careers, differently than those who might be apprehensive about how to make sense of information and articulate the way that learning can inform problem-solving.

Being critical, creative and flexible in the approach to social work education is, however, hard. The growing numbers of books and journal articles mark a new stage in our understanding and ability to make sense of the **knowledge**, **values** and **skills** required for practice. Accordingly, some social work students ponder how they can possibly be expected to cope with and prove that they have understood all the **laws**, **policies**, research and theories relevant to social work in their **assessments**. Of course, this is not an easy question, but it is worth remembering that those professional bodies that regulate social work practice provide a general consensus that to practise as a safe and effective social worker, students should first equip themselves with the **critical thinking** skills necessary to know what knowledge to apply in any given circumstance. It is not surprising, therefore, that there is growing attention to developing critical thinking and the intellectual potential of student social workers as a strict condition of their entry into the social work profession (Akintayo et al., 2016).

Recognising the need for social work students to develop critical thinking as a prerequisite to practice, this opening chapter introduces the main theories that underpin this skill. Acknowledging the fact that critical thinking is indeed a skill, which varies from one person to another and requires practice to develop, this chapter provides several exercises that you can adapt to guide and develop your confidence as an independent critical thinker as you study and then go on to practise social work.

As you proceed through this chapter it needs to be made clear that critical thinking should not be confused with being argumentative or being critical of other people. Although critical thinking skills can be used to expose limitations in some reasoning, arguments or conclusions, critical thinking can also play an important role in helping you to acquire knowledge, improve your own approach to practice and strengthen the arguments and recommendations that you make. When used to good effect, critical thinking could enhance your ability to promote social change, **anti-oppressive practice**, social cohesion, the empowerment and liberation of people and social work processes and the improvement of social institutions.

Critical thinking

Critical thinking is one of the most sought-after skills in social work, and is the ability to analyse information objectively and make a reasoned judgement. Effective critical thinking involves the ability to evaluate sources of knowledge, such as law, policy, research and theories, to draw and articulate reasonable and verifiable conclusions. It also requires an ability to discriminate between useful and less useful information to solve problems and to make decisions. Before moving on to explore the theories that underpin critical thinking in much more detail, it may be helpful to start off with an exercise. This exercise, detailed in Box 1.1, is aimed at encouraging you to begin to articulate your knowledge of social work from an individual and societal perspective. It tries to enable you to begin to flex your critical thinking skills as you consider social work and the values that underpin it from a fresh perspective.

 **Box 1.1 Activity**

The stranger at the bus stop

You are talking to a stranger at a bus stop who is frustrated about the late-running service. After a short time, the stranger asks you what you do for a living. You tell the stranger that you are a student social worker. The stranger, having never heard of a social worker before, becomes confused and turns to you for help. The stranger asks you the following five questions. Critically think about each question and then write down a detailed summary of what your response might be:

1. What is a student social worker?
2. Why do we need social workers?
3. Why is social work so important that it needs to be studied?
4. If there are social workers, why is there still discrimination and poverty?
5. What would happen if there were no social workers in the world?

When you have finished writing, carefully read each response that you gave to each question. Try to identify how much of your answer is informed by your opinion. Then try to identify how much of your answer is informed by the knowledge that has been gathered from, or generated by, empirical, theoretical or existential evidence.

    If your responses are informed by empirical, theoretical or existential evidence then your approach to critical thinking is clearly developing. You should use the exercises provided in this chapter to further develop that skill. However, if your responses were driven more by opinion, it is important that you use the exercises given below to devise a strategy to articulate your knowledge in a way that is free from personal or societal bias.

In our collective experience of doing and teaching social work, there appears to be a myth among some students that 'knowing' how to do social work is enough to practise. If a student has sufficient knowledge of the law, social policy, research and theories, the ability to do social work must follow. In practice, however, the relationship between knowledge and action is not so straightforward. We must remember that social work is, first and foremost, a relationship-based activity (Beresford et al., 2008). Most social workers work best when they are working with people. Yet because people are so amazingly unique, diverse and different, social workers must 'know' how to work effectively to validate and respect each person in an equal and inclusive way. This does not mean that social workers treat all people in the same way; it means that they work in different ways with different people according to individual need. For this reason, a social worker must know what laws, policies, research, theories and methods to apply, but they must also have the **practice wisdom** or method to know whether to apply this knowledge or not.

According to Klein and Bloom (1995: 799) *practice wisdom* is defined as 'a personal and value-driven system of knowledge that emerges out of the transaction between the phenomenological experience of the client situation and the use of scientific information'. In other words, it is the ability to do social work by carefully drawing upon lived experiences as well as empirical, theoretical or existential evidence. Being able to recite a section of the law, social policy, research, theories and methods is important, but this knowledge does not always help a social worker to do social work. Knowing the various details of the Care Act 2014, for instance, does not enable a person to conduct an assessment, to make decisions, to work with multi-agency teams, to manage conflict and distress or to confidently predict **risk**, **capacity**, vulnerability or **resilience**.

Danger point

Critical thinking is not a matter of accumulating and then remembering information. A person with a good memory and who knows a lot of facts may not necessarily be good at critical thinking. A critical thinker can deduce consequences from what is known and how things are known (that is called the epistemological basis of knowledge) but is also able to make use of information to solve problems and to disprove or verify any conclusions that are drawn. Knowing laws, social policies (those documents that help us interpret and apply law), research, theories and methods is one thing; but having the practice wisdom to know whether to apply this knowledge or not is another. To develop practice wisdom, social workers have to value the perspectives of **experts by experience**. They must ensure that the perspectives of each person involved in the decision-making processes are used to influence the way that social work is and is not done.

While knowledge of the law, social policy, eligibility thresholds, assessment tools, social work theories and methods is important, it can only serve as an important mandatory guide, or aide-memoire to inform practice. Law, social policy, eligibility thresholds, assessment tools, social work theories and methods do not always detail how social work should be done with every individual. The real work (and underlying detail of practice wisdom) is being able to apply knowledge but at the same time being able to work effectively and safely to understand how an individual, family or community is unique, diverse and different, to analyse what action is needed, and to create meaningful and effective projects of work that aim to empower, enable and liberate (Veal et al., 2016). What is more, the social worker must be able to apply their knowledge to promote the empowerment, enablement and liberation of others by rejecting, or at least being aware of, personal or societal bias. Law, social policy, eligibility thresholds, assessment tools, social work theories and methods do not always provide direction on how to achieve this.

The dangers of drawing upon generally sweeping or stereotypical conclusions can be shown in the conceptual examples of pathologising and **cultural relativist** approaches to practice that pepper our professional history. Together they highlight and reinforce the central importance of critical thinking. A much more detailed account of pathologising and cultural relativist approaches to practice will be provided in Chapter 6, but for this introduction, a brief explanation of both these **concepts** is necessary to provide a foundation of understanding that will permeate each subsequent page of this book.

Pathologising and cultural relativist practice

Let us be clear that pathologising practice and cultural relativist practice dangerous and unacceptable. This is because these approaches to practice threaten to undermine the social work profession by jeopardising the safety of the people you are training to support and the credibility of the social work profession.

Pathologising practice exists in those situations where social workers view or characterise a person as being medically or psychologically abnormal (Allen, 2018). Where pathologising practice occurs, a social worker undermines the importance of critical thinking and overlooks the need to work in different ways with different people. If we consider the overrepresentation of Black men in mental health services, or the overrepresentation of mothers living with a learning disability who have experienced the removal of a child into care, or the overrepresentation of single parents from low socio-economic backgrounds in child protection, for instance, it is also possible to consider how Black men, women living with a learning disability and people living in poverty are often labelled as 'trouble-makers', 'challenging', 'hard to reach' or worse. This pathologising reaction ignores the impact of **structural inequality** and oppression as any perception of 'risk' is heightened by an individual's stereotypical value judgements (Krumer-Nevo, 2016). These stereotypical judgements are then used to silence any opportunity for critical thinking to justify the various projects of social control. In addition to an increased use of statutory intervention, there follows the use of defensive social work procedures that focus on a person's perceived weaknesses, rather than on their available strengths. Without critical thinking, pathologising reactions in social work reduce wider perspectives, including the perspectives of the experts by experience, to narrow populist assumptions which reinforce oppression.

Pathologising reactions sit at one extreme on the scale of social work practice. At the other extreme of the scale is cultural relativism. Cultural relativism, in contrast to pathologising reactions, is the uncritical and devoted orientation towards anti-discrimination in obligation and duty. Where the importance of critical thinking is minimised or avoided, cultural relativism becomes manifest in a practitioner's reticence towards establishing the basis for intervention, even when intervention might

Danger point

The 'rule of optimism' was defined by Dingwall et al. (1995) to describe the occasion when a social worker, or any other allied health and social care professional, confuses an apparent willingness to comply with an actual willingness to accept the need to change. This confusion can lead professionals to minimise risk and undermine the importance of critical thinking. Even where the facts show that risk is ongoing or increasing, professionals can tell themselves that the opposite is true.

be necessary. Shown in the series of tragic outcomes reported in many serious case reviews, including those published after the death of Victoria Climbié in 2000, after the death of Daniel Pelka in 2012, and again in almost every serious case review that has been written, social workers and multi-agency teams who assess individuals, families and communities through a cultural relativist lens often collude with the **'rule of optimism'** (Dingwall et al., 1995).

Cultural relativism and the 'rule of optimism' are strongest when a social worker decides not to become involved in the lives of others because they refuse to believe that social work intervention is necessary. They have low expectations of the people they are working to support and normalise the situations that they assess against rising thresholds and shrinking resources (Allen and Riding, 2018).

To reduce the risks associated with pathologising or cultural relativist reactions, safe and effective practice requires social workers to ensure, as far as possible, that any decision to act, or not, is based upon verifiable fact, rather than on societal or personal prejudice. For this reason, the safest and most effective social worker knows that they must work in an anti-oppressive way (because that is what professional codes and theoretical principles tell them), but they can also articulate and substantiate with confidence how and why they work in an anti-discriminatory way. Being able to think and to think critically is therefore a requisite condition of avoiding pathologising or cultural relativist reactions. It is a skill that depends on the ability to apply **analysis**, logic and reason to the critical use of information. It requires you to question perceived knowledge as you reject anecdotal or non-scientific evidence to closely examine the source of all information. As we shall now see, and as will be developed in much more detail in subsequent chapters, critical thinking means thinking in a self-regulated and self-corrective manner.

Theories to inform critical thinking

The ability to think (and the ability to think about something) should be familiar to all of us. We can demonstrate the ability to think at those times when we need to make careful choices about what we do, what we wear, what we say to a friend who is upset and so on. Thinking involves the use of keen skills that require us to gather relevant information (independently or with the help of others) and to seek a solution to the issues with which we are grappling. Sometimes the solutions might be right, other times the solution might be wrong. In any case, experience enables us to learn, adapt and develop as thinkers as we try to make sense of the world around us.

Critical thinking, on the other hand, requires a deeper understanding of the problems or situations that we are faced with. It requires us to try to keep an open mind about different approaches and perspectives. It requires us to think reflectively rather than rushing to accept a situation or carry out a task without first taking time to fully understand or evaluate it. To think critically, or to learn how to solve any problem or learn any new knowledge, requires a person to take an active role in their own learning. Enabling an awareness of self is a key element of reflective social work practice that will be discussed further in Chapter 5.

Historically, conceptualisations of critical thinking have drawn on both theories of cognition in psychology and theories of reasoning in philosophy. The theories of cognition in psychology present various theories and views describing how thinking develops across the life course. It is impossible to present these views within the constraints of this short chapter, so the best-known views, summarised under the broad theoretical concepts of behaviourism, cognitivism, constructivism, **social constructivism**, metacognition, and an individual's motivation to learn are presented below (see Box 1.2).

--- ꀊꀉ --- Box 1.2   Theory explained ========================

Behaviourism is often simply referred to as 'learning theory'. It defines a person's ability to learn from observable behaviour that is reinforced through a stimulus–response related process. Behaviourism has a particular application in social work education, for example, in the way that effective critical thinking, writing, reading and reflection are often rewarded and then sought out through higher module marks.

Cognitivism is an aspect of psychology that focuses on ways in which people process information, including how people perceive, think, remember, learn, and solve problems. Cognitivism has an application in social work education, for example, in the way that students can gain **theoretical knowledge** at university and then apply and test this knowledge on placement.

Constructivism is a process in which the learner actively constructs new ideas or concepts based on their current and past experiences. Learning, therefore, is a personal endeavour. Constructivism has an application in social work education, for example, in the way that students can devise and promote the customisation of their own learning tasks according to prior knowledge, current life circumstances and aspirations for the future.

Social constructivism is the emphasis that is placed on the cultural context and social interactions that shape and inform thinking. In social constructivist terms, knowledge has a social nature and it is the result of social interaction and the use of language. Social constructivism has an application in social work education, for example, an emphasis on demonstrating core social work competencies at all times; not just when in University or

(Continued)

(Continued)

on placement. Here the doing of social work becomes more of a priority than memorising law, policy or theory.

Metacognition is often simply defined as the process of planning, assessing, and monitoring one's own thinking to develop understanding or self-regulation. Metacognition has an application in social work education, for example, in the way that students are expected to be effective self-managing learners and to reflect on their learning and developing social work practice.

Philosophically, John Dewey's (1991) emphasis on the connection between behaviourism, cognitivism, constructivism, social constructivism, metacognition, and experiential learning is at the heart of most definitions of the term 'critical thinking'. Thus, according to Dewey (1991), if a social work student is to master the skill of critical thinking, they should also seek opportunities to extend their education beyond the classroom, partaking in the scientific process of learning directly from the doing and reflecting on social work practice for real.

In summary, critical thinking is a form of reflective reasoning that analyses and evaluates information and arguments by applying a range of intellectual skills to reach clear, logical and coherent judgements within a given context. Student social workers must understand the language of reasoning and use different patterns of reasoning (including behaviourism, cognitivism, constructivism, social constructivism and metacognition), as well as different standards for evaluating arguments, in the diverse range of settings within which they work. To cultivate the ability to think critically, and to expand the knowledge and skills needed to become motivated to solve problems, student social workers must take an active role in their own learning. To carry out safe, verifiable and effective assessments, student social workers also do well to call on a variety of active thinking processes and should always seek to learn to see things from multiple points of view, including the lived experiences of the people who they are working to support. A safe, verifiable and effective assessment cannot occur in the absence of knowledge. In the same way, knowledge cannot produce a verifiable and effective assessment in the absence of skill. For this reason, student social workers need to learn the knowledge that underpins and guides social work, but they also need to think critically about how and when this information should be used.

For these reasons, which we hope are now obvious, student social workers require knowledge of how to do social work in theory, but they need to be able to reflect on, evaluate and apply this knowledge too. Knowledge of law, social policy, research and theories is important, but it can become meaningless if it is applied without 'practice wisdom' or a carefully considered method. We will now go on to consider which methods could be implemented to develop critical thinking skills.

Becoming a critical thinker: Bloom's taxonomy

In 1956, Benjamin Bloom, with collaborators Max Englehart, Edward Furst, Walter Hill, and David Krathwohl, published a framework for enabling the development of critical thinking skills. This framework is familiarly known as Bloom's taxonomy.

Bloom's taxonomy (Bloom et al., 1956) consisted of six major categories related to critical thinking. These were 'knowledge', 'comprehension', 'application', 'analysis', 'synthesis', and 'evaluation'. Supporting the previous discussions, the categories listed after 'knowledge' are presented as intellectual skills and abilities. By situating skills and abilities in this way, Bloom's taxonomy emphasised the understanding that knowledge is and should be the necessary precondition for putting critical thinking skills and abilities into practice.

While each category contains subcategories, all lying along a continuum from simple to complex and from concrete to abstract, the taxonomy is popularly remembered according to the six main categories presented in Figure 1.1.

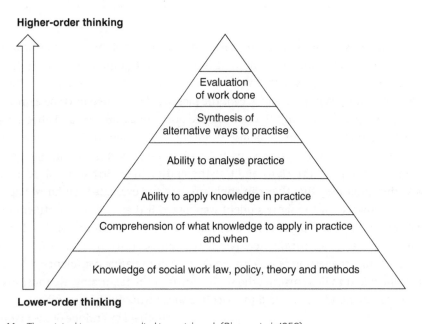

Higher-order thinking

Evaluation
of work done

Synthesis of
alternative ways to practise

Ability to analyse practice

Ability to apply knowledge in practice

Comprehension of what knowledge to apply in practice
and when

Knowledge of social work law, policy, theory and methods

Lower-order thinking

Figure 1.1 The original taxonomy applied to social work (Bloom et al., 1956)

In 2001, Lorin Anderson, a former student of Bloom, and David Krathwohl revisited the cognitive domains of Bloom's taxonomy and made some changes to the original model, including changing the categories from noun to verb forms (Anderson and Krathwol, 2001). Bloom's revised taxonomy (see Box 1.3) reflected a more active form of critical thinking and is perhaps more appropriate for social work education that promoted the application of critical thinking in a more practical way. As a result, this revised taxonomy is often used to underpin the way that your essays and assignments will be planned, structured and assessed. For more information on critical writing, see Chapter 3.

— ☼💡☼ **—** Box 1.3   Key point **━━━━━━━**

Bloom's revised taxonomy

- The noun 'evaluation' was replaced with the verb 'creating'
- The noun 'synthesis' was replaced with the verb 'evaluating'
- The noun 'analysis' was replaced with the verb 'analysing'
- The noun 'application' was replaced with the verb 'applying'
- The noun 'comprehension' was replaced with the verb 'understanding'
- The noun 'knowledge' was replaced with the verb 'remembering'.

Where have you seen the verbs listed above before? As you will see in Chapter 3, these verbs often form the basis of the **learning outcomes** that you will be assessed against. Why do you think that is?

As influential as Bloom's taxonomy has been in the development of critical thinking (and on your social work education), it is not without limitations. One of the main restrictions of the taxonomy is that it oversimplifies the nature of thought and its relationship to learning. While we can accept the fact that knowledge must be gained prior to going out on placement, and that knowledge does not assure safe and effective practice, it is likely that the ability to demonstrate the skills listed in the taxonomy might be altered depending on the context within which the person is working. If a student were asked to complete the skills audit at the end of their first work placement, for instance, they might say that they can apply, analyse and evaluate their knowledge with confidence. However, if the same student were asked if they still feel confident during the first week of a second placement, they might say no. The reason for this difference could lie in a change in confidence, familiarity and security that the student might experience. If this suggestion is true, we could say with relative confidence that to be a critical thinker and to demonstrate the skills shown in the taxonomy, we must first feel confident, familiar and safe to do and articulate social work in the first place.

Danger point

While Bloom's taxonomy is helpful in understanding the process of applying knowledge, it does not hold well against research or anti-oppressive theories. As any structure that claims to operate as a hierarchy can create a hierarchy, there is a degree of risk that Bloom's taxonomy could be used by some people to pathologise the intellectual abilities and skills of others.

Another key critique of the taxonomy can be found in the separation, or hierarchy, that is created between each 'skill' level. As the ability to think critically stems from a strictly linear progression, the model argues that individuals must become skilled at each distinct stage before moving up to the next level. Yet, we know through experience that sometimes it is harder to remember the theories that underpin relationship-based practices than it is to create long-lasting relations with others. Equally, we know that it can be more difficult to understand the behaviours and motivations of people we have worked to support than to evaluate the impact and success of our individual practice.

To demonstrate this critique further, use the activity detailed in Box 1.4. In this activity, we have used Bloom's revised taxonomy to produce a rudimentary skills audit. You might find that your confidence to demonstrate the skills listed does not follow the linear progression that the revised model suggests. You might also find that there are some skills that you would like to develop. For this reason, you should not abandon or devalue the taxonomy because of any critique offered here, but you could use it to devise a strategy for your own personal development.

 Box 1.4   Activity

Bloom's taxonomy skills audit

Table 1.1   A critical reflection skills audit

Category	Activity	I can demonstrate this skill with ease	I need to work on this skill	I struggle to demonstrate this skill	What do I need to do to maintain or develop this skill?
Remembering: Ability to recall or retrieve previously learned information	I can recall and describe with confidence the fundamental assumptions of at least six social work theories				
	I can retain and describe my knowledge of the law and policies to others				
	I can recite the core fundamental assumptions of social work to my tutor				
	I can describe the difference between a theory and a method				
Understanding: Ability to comprehend the meaning, translation, and interpretation of instructions and problems	I understand the meaning of evidence-based practice				
	I can apply my knowledge of social work law, policy, theory and method to practice				
	I can explain how I would work to promote the core tenets of anti-oppressive practice				

(Continued)

Table 1.1 (Continued)

Category	Activity	I can demonstrate this skill with ease	I need to work on this skill	I struggle to demonstrate this skill	What do I need to do to maintain or develop this skill?
	I can interpret complex theory and begin to apply it to hypothetical examples of practice				
	I can debate the difficulties associated with applying evidence-based practice				
Applying: Ability to use a concept in a new situation or unprompted use of an abstraction. Ability to apply what was learned in university on placement	I can begin to decide what social work theories and methods might be best to use in different situations				
	I can apply what I have learnt in university on placement with careful confidence				
Analysing: Ability to separate information into component parts	I can carry out detailed assessments and analyse information effectively				
	I can distinguish between fact and opinion				
Evaluating: Ability to make judgements about the value of ideas or materials	I can make good judgements about the value of my work, ideas and progress				
	I value constructive feedback from others (including feedback on my essays)				
Creating: Ability to make sense of complex information to make reliable recommendations for social work practice and policy	I can analyse information to identify patterns				
	I can draw upon a wide range of information to create a reliable understanding of situations and the difficulties that others may be having				
	I can effectively assess, measure and manage risk, capacity, vulnerability and resilience				
	I can influence local social work policy and practice				

As in the original version, the six categories listed in Table 1.1 can be thought of as degrees of difficulty. Make a note of those skills that you can demonstrate with ease, those that you might need to work on and those that you struggle to demonstrate. Given that categories listed below can be thought of as degrees of difficulty, what do you think you need to do to say, 'I can demonstrate every skill with ease'?

Since the publication of Bloom's taxonomy, others have attempted to update and improve on that initial effort. For social work, the most obvious and pertinent taxonomies can be found in the professional codes of practice that underpin the need for **critical reflection** and **critical analysis** in particular.

Critical reflection and analysis

The ability to apply critical reflection and analysis to inform and provide a rationale for professional decision-making is a core condition of professional social work practice. Consistent with one principle of Bloom's taxonomy, that knowledge must precede action, the International Federation of Social Workers (IFSW) Global Standards for the Education and Training of the Social Work Profession (2014) require professional social workers to be able to apply the principles of critical thinking and reasoned discernment. Social workers are expected to identify, distinguish, evaluate and integrate multiple sources of knowledge and evidence to use critical thinking in a way that is augmented by creativity and curiosity. But unlike Bloom's taxonomy, the IFSW acknowledges the fact that critical thinking is both a generic capability and a very specific skill, that is developed in particular contexts. According to the IFSW (2014) effective critical thinking can:

- Measure the impact/value of practice on the people you are training to support
- Encourage practitioners to value and consider diverse knowledge sources
- Improve an individual's ability to evaluate why good practice is facilitated or hindered
- Highlight the importance of supervision and critical reflection
- Challenge and maintain curiosity, creativity and self-awareness.

Honing critical thinking skills requires time, energy and effort. It takes practice. Yet, while the IFSW (2014) makes clear why effective critical thinking is important, it does not provide an equal amount of information about how to become a critical thinker.

In our experience as social work lecturers, one way that you can practise the skills required by the IFSW and other regulatory bodies and independent professional membership organisations for social work is to think about doing social work in three stages. The first stage is to identify the recommendation – those things that social work knowledge, values and skills recommended for practice. The second stage is to identify the barriers to achieving that recommendation. The third and final stage requires you to identify a potential solution to overcome those barriers. Often the second and third stages are repeated until no further barriers can be found to the solutions that are offered. An example of this three-stage model of critical thinking is detailed in Figure 1.2. The activity in Box 1.5 then encourages you to try out these three stages of critical thinking for yourself.

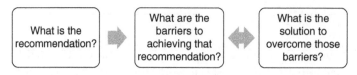

Figure 1.2   Three-stage model for critical reflection

Thinking on purpose: barriers and solutions

This exercise is designed to help you think laterally and discover new ways of looking at the world. Table 1.2 lists three proposed recommendations that concern social work. Using creative and constructive thinking, try to identify barriers (those things that might prevent the recommendation becoming a reality) and solutions (the answers to address or overcome the barriers) to the recommendations. Try to list as many barriers and solutions as you can, and stop when you can think of no more solutions to the barriers that you list.

Table 1.2

Recommendation	Barriers	Solutions
Every person should have a social worker who supports them		
No young person should ever suffer from adversity in childhood		
People who live with an enduring mental health difficulty should never have to experience discrimination		

How many barriers and solutions did you identify? Count your barriers and solutions for each recommendation and compare them to the scores below:

- If you managed to write more than 20 barriers and 20 solutions for each recommendation, well done – you may be an excellent critical thinker.
- If you managed to write less than 20 barriers and 20 solutions for each recommendation but managed to write more than 10 barriers and 10 solutions, well done – you may be a good critical thinker.

- If you managed to write less than 10 barriers and 10 solutions to each recommendation but managed to write more than 5 barriers and 5 solutions, well done – you may be a fair critical thinker.

Using the 'three-stage model for critical reflection' that we have developed above, try to consider other recommendations that are relevant to you and your own learning. For example, try to link the model to an upcoming assignment or a challenge that you are experiencing on placement. Regardless of the focus, try to structure your thinking around barriers and solutions until no further barriers can be found.

Recognising that critical reflection is a skill that varies from one person to another, we also appreciate the fact that while the 'three-stage model for critical reflection' may be useful to some, it may not be useful to others. A further method for critical thinking requires us to look outside of social work – in this case, to Edward de Bono and the field of educational psychology.

Becoming a critical thinker: Six Thinking Hats®

Nominated for the Nobel Prize in 2005, Edward de Bono is regarded by many as the leading authority in the field of critical thinking. One of his most famous and successful methods to promote and develop critical thinking is Six Thinking Hats. The method was first introduced in 1985 by Edward De Bono in a book with the same name.

Edward de Bono's (1985) Six Thinking Hats technique is another extremely useful way to structure critical thinking. It can be used to debate an issue, to solve a problem or to arrive at an important decision. The technique encourages a person to approach the problem, situation or focus of thought from six contrasting angles.

Because your social work education will be hard and as unique, diverse and different as the people you are training to support, you will certainly have to apply different thinking processes at each stage of your degree. If you do not apply different thinking processes, it could be that your social work judgements become prescriptive or difficult to substantiate. While pathologising and cultural relativism reactions are a real risk when critical thinking is absent, it might also be true to say that if you are working hard to plan an assignment but have not spent enough time reading the literature that is available, confusion and frustration will begin to characterise the work you do.

As we have already suggested, confusion, insecurity and a lack of confidence or familiarity are the biggest enemies of critical thinking. To avoid confusion, de Bono (1985) suggests thinking about wearing six metaphorical hats to direct and guide how you think. Instead of trying to do everything at once, de Bono (1985) recommends trying to learn to handle the different types of thinking one at a time. Using de Bono's (1985) six hats method, you will begin to learn that different thinking is needed in different situations. You can then focus your thinking deliberately in one direction.

The six thinking hats are grounded in de Bono's (1985) famous concept of 'lateral thinking' which requires a critical thinker to base a judgement on a comprehensive study of the different aspects of any issue separately. In the end, these different aspects come together to form critical thinking. In the six hats method, thinking is represented by six different coloured hats that are designed to help the thinker visualise the six different ways to think. We will return to the six hats model later in this book, but by identifying six modes of thinking we have begun to show how critical thinking is central to the task and process of social work. The Six Thinking Hats method is a useful way to mind-map solutions to overcome the barriers that you encounter in thinking about social work or in doing social work, as shown in the hypothetical example presented in Box 1.6.

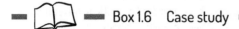 **Box 1.6   Case study**

Wearing de Bono's hats to overcome a challenge

Mandeep is a second-year social work student who is completing a module on human growth and development. The essay question for the module is: 'Attachment theory has gained great prominence in social work practice. Using empirical and theoretical evidence, critically evaluate whether this prominence is justified.'

Mandeep looks at the question and feels lost. She does not know where to start. She goes to see her personal tutor, who introduces her to de Bono's (1985) Six Think-ing Hats technique. The tutor explains that this is a good tool to begin to think more critically about the essay question. When she gets home, Mandeep puts each meta-phorical hat on in turn to complete the following task:

The white hat: logical planning

While wearing the white hat, Mandeep begins to think about how available infor-mation on attachment theory could help her to understand the topic. Questions she asked herself when using the white hat included:

- What information do I have about attachment theory?
- What information on other theories do I have?
- What does this information tell me?
- What information do I lack?
- What information would I like to have?
- How will I get this information?

The red hat: feelings, intuition and emotions

While wearing the red hat, Mandeep begins to write down and express her feelings, without having to offer a rational explanation, about her upcoming assignment. Feelings, intuition and emotions included:

- I feel frustrated that I don't know what to do
- Sometimes the things that people write on social media about what they are doing for essays make me feel inadequate
- I would be happy if I read more about attachment theory
- I feel confident to access resources from the library and online databases
- I feel worried that I will fail the assignment.

The black hat: caution and critical thinking

While wearing the black hat, Mandeep begins to consider any weak points in her previous approaches to studying. She tries to find an idea or solution to work out how to avoid or counter past mistakes. Caution and critical thinking induced:

- Sometimes I have left writing my essays until the last minute
- I don't do enough reading prior to writing
- I don't really understand what attachment theory is and what the alternatives are
- I need to improve my referencing
- I need to read more and plan my work more thoroughly.

The yellow hat: looking at the positives

While wearing the yellow hat, Mandeep tries to develop an optimistic but logical view of her strategy to pass the assignment. She tries to think about how feasible a new approach might be. Benefits and feasibility thoughts included:

- I must use the time that I have and my commitment to pass to read more widely
- I am usually a good planner. I can use these skills to plan my essay
- I want to be a good social worker. I can use this vocational commitment to succeed
- I can achieve great things if I put my mind to it.

The green hat: creativity, new ideas and possibilities

While wearing the green hat, Mandeep tries to seek new approaches and innovative solutions to the challenges that she is facing. Every idea is considered at this stage. Creativity, new ideas and possibilities included:

- I will book an appointment with the subject librarian
- I will visit the study skills team to develop my referencing skills
- I will set specific reading time each day so that I can research information for my essay
- I will set specific writing time each day so that I can plan and write my essay

(Continued)

(Continued)

- I will tell my friends that I am busy studying if they ask me out during my planned reading and writing time
- I will stay off social media until my assignment is done.

The blue hat: process control

While wearing the blue hat, Mandeep tries to summarise the whole thinking process. She reviews the answers and responses that she has given to examine her developing plan of action to see if any areas of thinking require revision. For example, she decided after reading her responses that she needed to return to some creative green hat thinking.

Working through the de Bono (1985) Six Thinking Hats model simply involves trying to switch between perspectives to consider or explore your problem from a different angle. Using the six hats will, of course, take practice. Each hat brings with it a very different approach to problem-solving. Clearly, understanding, knowing and remembering the role and objectives of each of the six hats in advance can help you to utilise them in more optimal ways as you work through your problem, so that you can begin to realise your potential as a critical thinker.

SUMMARY

To demonstrate critical thinking, it is important that you are knowledgeable about the principles of logic, scientific inquiry, and reasoned discernment. As you develop the confidence to do social work you should also build confidence to apply your critical thinking skills, augmented with creativity and curiosity. Critical thinking also requires you to be able to synthesise and talk about relevant information. You should be working hard to distinguish, appraise and integrate multiple sources of knowledge, including research-based knowledge, models of assessment, prevention, intervention and evaluation, but you will also develop the practice wisdom to know when and when not to apply this knowledge in practice.

Having read this chapter, you should be able to:

- Recognise the importance of critical reflection as a core social work skill
- Develop a strategy to develop your own critical reflection skills
- Use various methods of critical reflection to consider practice (and problems) form multiple positions
- Consider the value of critical reflection in pursuit of safe, effective and excellent social work practice.

FURTHER READING

de Bono, E. (1985). *Six Thinking Hats: An Essential Approach to Business Management.* Boston: Little, Brown, & Company.

Fook, J. and Askeland, G. A. (2007). Challenges of critical reflection: 'Nothing ventured, nothing gained'. *Social Work Education, 26*(5), 520–533.

2

INTRODUCTION TO CRITICAL KNOWLEDGE

.... THEORETICAL BACKGROUND

- Learning outcomes and QAA/HCPC
- Benchmarking and verification of knowledge
- Critical reflection to demonstrate deep and extensive learning
- Applying critical thinking
- Evidencing, evaluating and synthesising knowledge

.... RELEVANCE TO SOCIAL WORK THINKING AND PRACTICE

- Verification of knowledge
- Analysis, evaluation and synthesis
- Theory to understand and theory to inform decision-making
- General knowledge

.... REAL-WORLD CHALLENGES

- Lack of understanding in terms of different knowledge forms (research, theory, experiential, etc.)
- Limitations in ability to apply theory and knowledge to real-world situations
- Demands of the job mean that knowledge is applied uncritically

Introduction

In this chapter we will build upon the concepts, tools and strategies that have been presented in Chapter 1. By enabling you to understand what is meant by 'knowledge', and by prompting you to question the value and application of different types of knowledge, we consider the foundation of critical thinking in more detail. By establishing the basis of using theoretical and empirical knowledge to inform practice, rather than as something that might be associated with practice in hindsight, this chapter will begin to develop your awareness of the importance of working in a systematic and evidence-informed way. Using knowledge in this way will enable you to be the best social worker that you can possibly be, using a variety of knowledge to underpin what you do, how you do it, what decisions you make and why.

It is crucial, however, that you approach this chapter with a critical lens. That is, that you take a questioning approach; knowledge, whatever its form, should not be taken for granted and accepted without some consideration of its limitations and the potentially narrow contexts in which it has emerged. For example, all knowledge is in time and space. In other words, it has been produced at a particular point in time and in a particular place with all sorts of influences. Factors such as the agenda of the political party in government, the philosophical 'flavour of the month', or even the source of research funding for a social problem may influence the direction of research and the ways in which it is reported.

The link between philosophy and knowledge

Debates about knowledge, in general, involve a consideration of **ontology** (the nature of existence and of reality) and **epistemology** (the nature of knowledge). Ontological questions concern the nature of reality by asking, for example, whether there is a 'real' world out there that is independent of our knowledge of it. As such, ontology is the study of how we determine if something exists or not. Refer to Chapter 1, where we introduced you to social constructivism. If you adopted a social constructivist ontology, you would believe that our knowledge of the world is socially constructed and results from social interactions in a cultural context. An example of this is given in Box 2.1.

Epistemology, on the other hand, is the study of knowledge and focuses on the methods of producing knowledge, its validity and scope, as well as the justification between knowledge, belief and opinion. Epistemological questions include:

- What is knowledge?
- How can we know anything?
- How can we know that we know?
- What can we know with certainty?
- How is belief different from knowledge?

The importance and relevance of epistemology lie in the need to understand the nature and scope of knowledge in terms of its application in practice. Maynard (1994: 100) sums this up when he claims that: 'Epistemology is concerned with providing a philosophical grounding for deciding what kind of knowledge are possible and how we can ensure that they are both adequate and legitimate'. In other words, in our everyday practice settings, we should strive to ensure that we are using the most reliable and appropriate sources of knowledge to inform our practice decisions and professional judgements to remain ethical and accountable.

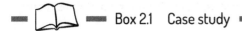 ■ Box 2.1   Case study ■

Constructions of 'good enough'

Thirty-year-old Tessa is a single parent of two children aged 12 and 5 years of age. She grew up in a poor inner-city area and her parents struggled with periods of unemployment and a low income. Yet childhood was a happy time for Tessa as she was loved by her parents and was often shown affection. She was a confident young person. She often went without the things that she would have liked (the latest fashionable clothes, make-up, etc.), but her friends grew up in similar households and they were all in the same boat. Tessa does not believe in spoiling her children or indulging them with expensive clothes. However, her 12-year-old son, Mark, wants the latest sportswear and trainers with brand labels. Tessa buys cheap, affordable clothing from local supermarkets, which she considers are 'good enough' for her children. Tessa and Mark have different ontological perspectives as Mark considers that he 'needs' certain clothing to be popular within his friendship group. Mark's friend Jordan wears all the latest sportswear and Mark believes that Tessa is not a good parent as she should get him what he wants too.

   Question: What perspective do you have on this issue? How is your perspective informed ontologically? (If not socially constructed, then refer back to the theoretical explainer in Box 1.2 in Chapter 1 and consider the other theories proposed there.)

Contexts for applying knowledge: the care versus control dichotomy

Before moving on to critically explore different forms of knowledge, it is important to locate these discussions within a broader question of whether the dual functions of social work – of 'care' and 'control' – are compatible, or if one supplants the other in the delivery of social work interventions. This is a complex and long-standing argument, but integral to the epistemological and ontological questions of knowledge and how it is employed in practice contexts. The notion that social work is a professional occupation underpinned by a controlling function is one which means that practitioners are tasked with enforcing rules and regulations through a 'rational-technical activity' (based upon an instrumental and procedural ethic) rather than a 'practical-moral activity' (a relationship-based and caring ethic) (Parton, 2000: 452). In the current climate of social work, which is largely driven by neoliberal principles (advocating a market economy, consumer choice, performance-driven indicators, etc.), the more rational-technical approach to social work would seem to displace a more practical-morally based profession. However, it is the latter which many argue, including Parton, that underpins social work **praxis** and, as such, this results in a disconnect between the neoliberal project and social work practice. This debate is intrinsically connected to the epistemological question of knowledge because rational-technical and practical-moral activities require different forms of knowledge.

Forms of knowledge

A logical starting point is to consider what we mean when we talk about 'knowledge'. In social work practice, you will draw from a range of knowledge forms to support your assessment, communication, judgements, decision-making, choice of intervention, partnership working and so on. But, what is this thing, that we call 'knowledge'? The *Oxford Living Dictionary* (OLD) defines knowledge as 'Facts, information, and skills acquired through experience or education; the theoretical or practical understanding of a subject' (OLD, 2018a). Trevithick (2012) wrote about three forms of knowledge for practice: theoretical knowledge; factual knowledge; and practical knowledge. There are, however, many different forms and sources of knowledge, and these are outlined in Table 2.1. In this chapter, we will consider various forms of knowledge and encourage you to view them through a critical lens in order to assess the value and limitations of each.

Table 2.1 Forms of knowledge

Knowledge type	Description
Local knowledge	This is knowledge of the local area and it might include information about communities or about services and other infrastructures (transport, local amenities, or projects)
Organisational knowledge	This results from information collected by your employer that informs the organisation and its staff about the locale or a particular group or community
Policy knowledge	Law and policy form a sizeable knowledge framework. Social workers need to know about the law and policy relevant to their area of practice: for example, knowledge of the Children Act 1989 for child protection social workers, or of the Care Act 2014 for adult social workers
Practitioner knowledge	This is knowledge gained through experience but could also be the knowledge that you have about a particular issue or about a person whom you are supporting for example. It might be knowledge held by your colleague who has specialist knowledge of a particular area of practice (e.g. a substance misuse specialist)
Research knowledge	Examples are current research articles and research reports. Research knowledge can be used to underpin practice judgements, decisions and interventions

Knowledge type	Description
Theoretical knowledge	In terms of theory, social work knowledge draws from a range of disciplines including sociology, psychology, counselling, law and social policy
User and carer knowledge (a.k.a. experts by experience)	Consider that every person you are training to support is an expert in their own life and situation and, as such, they hold important information that will inform social work practice. Do not neglect carers, as they too can hold important information that you need to make a full assessment

Source: Adapted from Rogers et al. (2016)

 **Box 2.2   Activity**

What type of knowledge?

Look at the sources of information in Table 2.2. What type of knowledge are they according to the categories in Table 2.1?

Table 2.2   Forms of Knowledge

Information	Type of knowledge
Six-year-old Craig has lived with a foster family for 2 years. Until the birth of his little brother, Wesley, Craig had regular contact with his birth mother (they have different fathers, and Craig does not see his father). Contact has become a little erratic and Craig's behaviour at home and at school has become a little disruptive at the same time.	
Crime rates in the community of Hat, in Glove Town, are 10% higher than the national average for young adults aged 18–25 and Glove Council has used these statistics in its 'Fighting Local Crime' strategy.	
Rogers's (1965) concept of the three core conditions of 'congruence', 'empathy' and 'unconditional positive regard' underpins this notion of person-centred practice.	
Section 120 of the Adoption and Children Act 2002 expands the notion of 'significant harm' in relation to domestic abuse to include harms experienced by directly or indirectly witnessing the ill-treatment or abuse of another.	

Theoretical knowledge

The social work literature is peppered with references to both 'knowledge' and 'theory', and sometimes these terms are used interchangeably. We would argue that theory is only one form of knowledge (as indicated above). It is, however, an important form of knowledge for social work education and praxis. Theory can be understood to be 'A supposition or a system of ideas', or a set of general principles that explain a particular thing (OLD, 2018b). An example is Einstein's theory of relativity. Thompson (2010) distinguishes between informal and formal theory, with the latter being more explicit and better defined than the former. Informal theory can be considered to be the beliefs, norms, perspectives and attitudes that people hold, while formal theory is much more explicit in its content and is subject to scientific and rigorous analysis and testing. Thompson (2010) observes that people can use formal theory, either directly or indirectly, to underpin or question the informal theory that they have about the world. In this way, both are blended with practice wisdom (discussed further below) in order to inform social work practice.

Social work as a discipline and a profession does not have its own set of social work theories, but it has evolved drawing from a range of theories, reflecting the complexity and diversity of social work practice. As a practitioner, you will use theories drawn from a variety of disciplines. See Box 2.3 for a brief definition of the most commonly used theories in praxis, but note that this is not a definitive list and there are lots of other disciplines and fields that can inform social work knowledge and practice (such as law, organisational theory, health-based knowledge, politics, economics, ethics and philosophy).

Box 2.3   Theory explained

Sociology. Broadly, this is the scientific study of society and social order/disorder. This includes the investigation of structure, formation and development of society as well as the study of the individual and their relation to the social world. Sociology includes the study of social problems, patterns of social relationships, social interaction and culture.

Psychology. This is the study of the human mind and human behaviour. This can include the study of the mentality and behaviour of individuals as well as groups. Psychology is a multidimensional discipline and includes many sub-fields, including such areas as human development, clinical psychology, health, social behaviour and cognitive processes.

Social policy. In essence, the study of social policy concerns an understanding of social and public policy and its functioning in society. Social policy is concerned with the ways in which the state (government) responds to social problems through policy and law initiatives in relation to a number of human needs such as security, education, employment, health and wellbeing. Social policy also explores how states and societies respond to global challenges of a social, demographic and economic nature.

Human growth and development theories. These are concerned with the study of the theory that explains how humans grow and develop through the life course from birth to death. Many psychological theories are drawn on here.

Communication. This embraces a range of theories that explore the principles and methods of communication in all its forms, whether it be between people, or people and machines, or other modes of transmittal.

Indeed, there is a vast amount of theory and it is helpful to categorise types of theory across a spectrum from informal theories borne out of experience (the type of theory that you can build from experience of working with a particular issue or specific group of people) to more formal grand theories which have emerged through scholarship to explain structural phenomena (see Figure 2.1). Each type of theory has benefits and limitations. For example, informal theory (including experiential knowledge) can be critiqued for its lack of generalisability, small body of substantiating evidence and situated context, whereas a grand theory can be useful in terms of analysing experience as shaped by society's embedded norms and values which are reinforced through institutions such as education or the legal framework. Grand theories can be rather deterministic in that their explanations may not account for an individual's unique situation, strengths, resilience and ability to create change which serve to dispute the very theory used to explain their situation! Angela's life story in Box 2.4 provides an example of this; Black feminist theory (a theoretical position that explains the oppression and discrimination of Black and minority ethnic women) might provide one interpretation of Angela's earlier life, but it would not necessarily explain Angela's achievements in adulthood.

Micro or informal theory, or experiential knowledge	Middle range theories	Grand theory, or grand narratives
Includes anecdotal knowledge, common-sense perspectives, attitudes or beliefs. In other words, theoretical knowledge generated from practice and real-world situations.	Like grand theories, these make claims using abstract ideas but generally focus on a particular issue (e.g., poverty or oppression).	Theories derived from abstract ideas which claim to provide comprehensive explanations covering the whole of society (e.g., feminist theory or Marxism).

Figure 2.1 A theoretical spectrum

 **Box 2.4   Case study**

Angela's story

Angela was brought up in a household in a Northern mill town in England. She had one younger brother, Edmund. She was the daughter of a local White British woman and a Somali man who had come to England in the 1960s as a young man looking for work and a place to call home. Her mother worked as a seamstress and her father was employed in a local factory. As a young person with a mixed heritage, life was not always easy for Angela as she encountered racism and bullying at school. Despite this, in early adulthood, she worked hard to contribute to the household and to get an education. She went to university, got a degree and then over the next twenty years she forged a successful career as a university lecturer, eventually achieving the status of professor and an expert in her field.

The function of theory varies too. Collingwood et al. (2008) distinguishes between two functions: theories to inform (how to make sense of the information that you have, and to identify what else you might need to know) and theories to intervene (to help decide what methods you are then going to use). In this way, theories help social workers to make sense of and understand situations as well as make decisions about moving forward (writing support plans, referring on to more appropriate support, etc.). There is a third function: theories can go beyond helping us to understand or describe why something has happened, and how we can respond to it, but theories can also help us to make predictions about the likelihood of something happening in any given situation (Trevithick, 2012). This is an important distinction when you are tasked with assessing and managing risk, because one of the things that you will need to consider is what could happen if you do *not* intervene. See Box 2.5 for a case study where theory has underpinned a piece of work.

 **Box 2.5   Case study**

Miguel's story

At the age of 22 years, Miguel was a care leaver. He had just left university after gaining a degree in sports science. Miguel had grown up in foster care and was lucky to have stayed with the family since he was placed with them when he was 9 years of age. There was one issue, though, that caused Miguel significant upset; he had not seen his brother, Paulo, since he was 15 years old. This was due to a decision made at the time for the benefit of both brothers after they had had a considerable falling-out. However, Miguel had an enduring sense of something missing from his life as he had been close to his brother (they had lived with separate foster families, but this was the only contact Miguel had with someone from his birth family). Miguel's social worker, Rick, drew on Kübler-Ross's (1969) five stages of grief theory to make sense of Miguel's ongoing psychological and emotional state centring on this loss, and Rick concluded that Miguel had not reached the final stage of 'acceptance'. Rick also employed systems theory to help him to understand the impact of this on Miguel. Briefly, systems theory proffers the idea that a 'system' is made up of several parts, and if the parts do not work well together, then the system is out of balance and does not work as it should. Its functioning is impaired and balance (homeostasis) is lost. Rick considered that the family system constituted by Miguel and Paulo's relationship needed an intervention to restore homeostasis and enable the relationship (and that family system) to be repaired. Rick arranged for mediation to help the brother renew their relationship. After a series of mediation sessions, Miguel and Paulo's relationship was restored. The system was back in working order and Miguel was able to move on from his feelings of loss.

User and carer knowledge

As explained in the Introduction, in this book we avoid the label 'user' and employ 'expert by experience' or just refer to the people you are training to support. These individuals are key stakeholders in social work practice, as their narratives offer important sources of knowledge. Encouraging their involvement is not just good practice, but integral to *effective* practice. Furthermore, it is embedded in various pieces of law, policy and statutory regulations. For example, the Children Act 1989 specifies that social workers should consult with children to ascertain their 'wishes and feelings'. In adult social work, the Care Act 2014 guides interventions and also includes a clause stating that people should be consulted in order to understand their wishes, feelings and beliefs. Just because these requirements are integrated within the law, it does not mean that the collaborative process of obtaining this information is easy. Quite often some people might be reluctant to engage with social work practitioners, whether based on previous experiences, fear and apprehension, or other causes of resistance. It is, however, important that we strive to integrate the narratives of experts by experience as central forms of knowledge in our assessment, planning and interventions, and in-service delivery reviews and evaluations on a grander scale (Davies and Gray, 2017).

Some areas of practice, more so than others, have successfully adopted the approach of considering people to be 'experts by experience', including adult social work with people with learning disabilities. Beresford (2000: 493; emphasis in the original) notes that this type of knowledge 'based on *direct* experience' should counter and balance social work interventions which concurrently utilise other forms of knowledge (both theoretical and practice-based).

Danger point: using theory uncritically

You should remember that there is no theory that is 'one-size-fits-all'. Therefore, just as a theory will have its strengths and value, it will also have its limitations. For example, Rick found a solution using systems theory to understand what was going on and to inform his decision-making. But if Paulo had been unwilling to engage in a series of mediation sessions, then this would not have been a successful outcome and Rick would have had to think of another way of helping Miguel. Some theories will require the cooperation of others to be effective, particularly theories or models built on the principles of working in partnership.

Danger point: barriers to integrating 'user and carer' knowledge

If we value the knowledge to be gleaned from experts by experience then this will be at the core of social work assessments, planning and interventions. If not, and if collecting these narratives can be described as being tokenistic, it will be evident that assessments, planning and interventions are not based on this knowledge, but on other forms of knowledge. Not only this, it may be that other factors may become organisational constraints (local policy, lack of capacity within services, lack of available specialist service provision, threshold criteria, lack of resources, problems with access, etc.) which might override the implications that can be drawn from the knowledge offered by experts by experience in terms of the need for interventions.

Question: What might the solution be to minimise or counter some of these barriers?

Tacit knowledge

Polyani (1967) coined the term **'tacit knowledge'** to capture the notion that this type of knowledge can be difficult to communicate to another person as it is not known explicitly. An example of tacit knowledge is the ability to speak a language. How can you explicitly transfer the knowledge of this to another person? The concept of tacit knowledge is similar to intuition; both are rather mysterious and ephemeral but noted as important throughout the social work literature. Schön (1983: viii) clarified this point, noting that tacit knowledge is 'knowing in practice' or, as Osmond (2005: 884) termed it, 'unconscious knowing'.

 — Box 2.6 Activity

Can you think of examples of tacit knowledge, that is, knowledge that is difficult to write down, visualise or transfer to another person?

Evidence-based practice

Evidence-based practice (EBP) can be defined as an approach which advocates the use of evidence that has been collected in a systematic and rigorous way to inform decision-making. Kiteley and Stogdon (2014: 142) use the term 'evidence-based practice' to describe 'social work practice that is informed by academically-tested knowledge and has credibility across social work disciplines'. MacDonald (2008: 435) offers an alternative view centred upon outcomes:

> when professionals intervene in people's lives they should do so on the basis of the best available evidence regarding the likely consequences of their actions. Put simply, they should be as confident as possible that what they do will (1) bring about the changes sought, and (2) will do so without adverse consequences.

MacDonald makes important points about the use of 'best available evidence' to bring about a change, as well as avoiding negative outcomes. Lindsay (2007) proffers a similar view, but notes the importance of transparency. These arguments are difficult to dispute, but the very notion of EBP has triggered various debates. This section will not go into detail, but serves to introduce you to the notion of EBP and some of the debates surrounding it.

One of the complexities surrounding EBP debates is similar to some of the points made in this chapter with questions around what constitutes knowledge and what counts as valid knowledge. In Box 2.7 you are asked to think about types of evidence. Broadly speaking, evidence is anything that is presented to prove or disprove an assertion. It is closely linked to epistemology, and the historical background to EBP is

— 🖐 — Box 2.7   Activity ━━━━━━━━━━━━━━━━━

Reflecting on the use of evidence

Think about the types of evidence that you use in your everyday decision-making. This could be in a situation that you have encountered in a social care or related post, or in your personal life (such as making a decision about where to go on holiday). What evidence do you use? Is it anecdotal (that is, your friend told you something), theoretical or empirical (derived from past and provable from experience or research)? Which do you think is the most reliable? Do you feel confident in describing the evidence? Do you feel confident in justifying your decision using this evidence?

Now think about your last visit to a GP or hospital. Would you be happy if a decision were made about your treatment that was not based on evidence (that is, science), but was more of a 'gut feeling' that something might work to make you better? Would that be acceptable to you? Can we compare one profession with another (medicine with social work)? Your immediate instinct might be to say 'yes', but social and medical situations are very different. Social workers work with social, health, psychological and economic factors. The same problem in two different locations (England and China, for example) might need very different responses, but the same medical diagnosis for two people in two different locations (England and China) would likely require the same treatment.

---

mostly tied to a positivist epistemology (see Box 2.8) and a 'what works' framework (Dominelli, 2005). Webb (2006) usefully points out that the discourse of EBP within a positivist **paradigm** unhelpfully neglects the centrality of reflection and its place in the practice of social work. Exploring the background and underpinning philosophies of EBP, Webb also notes how the scientific, rigorous research approach to EBP fits well with the neoliberal tools and techniques (market and target-driven practices, for example) that have influenced the structure and function of social work in recent years. EBP has its origins in medicine, and this may account for its epistemological and ontological underpinning which favours a positivistic paradigm. Conversely, the 'what works' approach has a tendency to neglect and reject non-positivist ways of knowledge production, while the more contemporary research tradition of the social work profession advocates smaller-scale, qualitative projects (Dominelli, 2005).

— 🖐 — Box 2.8   Theory explained ━━━━━━━━━━━━━━━━━

Positivism is a philosophical theory which adopts the view that certain knowledge is based on *natural* phenomena and their attributes and relations. Society, like the physical world, operates in accordance with general laws which are observable and verifiable.

(Continued)

(Continued)

In other words, both the physical world and social reality are independent of those who observe them. Furthermore, positivists believe that information derived from sensory experience, interpreted through reason and logic, forms the *exclusive* source of all certain knowledge and, as such, verified data (positive facts) received from the senses are considered to be **empirical evidence** (and thus, positivism is based on **empiricism**).

In their discussion of EBP, Kiteley and Stogdon (2014) illuminate the problem caused by mass media reactions to tragedies (for example, high-profile child deaths such as that of Peter Connelly) as public and political responses assume that a 'common-sense' approach to social work practice should be the way in which the profession manages similar cases to avoid the similar tragedies. The very notion of a 'common-sense' approach moves significantly away from a positivist approach to EBP. Yet, the notion that scientific research provides the most reliable and legitimate evidence prevails. Arguably, there is a hierarchy of evidence, with particular types of research (randomised controlled trials and systematic reviews) considered to be the gold standard of research design (Rubin and Bellamy, 2012).

Recent debates have advocated for more qualitative research and practice evidence to be included in EBP to counter the formulaic, prescriptive nature of positivistic approaches which can neglect the uniqueness of both the people you are training to support and social work practitioners (Gray et al., 2009). These debates have progressed with a slightly different conception and terminology offered as an alternative: that of **evidenced-informed practice** (EIP). Epstein (2009: 224) argues for EIP by noting that 'practice knowledge and intervention decisions might be enriched by prior research but not limited to it. In this way, EIP is more inclusive than EBP'. Epstein and others have advocated for EIP, noting how it holds the potential to be more integrated and inclusive and, importantly, allows for the addition of **user and carer knowledge** by paying attention to their views and experiences. It can also include the other forms of knowledge discussed in this chapter.

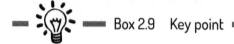 Box 2.9   Key point

The professional framework and EBP/EIP

- The Professional Capabilities Framework states that social workers should 'make use of research to inform practice'.
- The Knowledge and Skills Statement (DfE, 2014) for child and family practitioners states that social workers should 'make use of the best evidence from research to ... support families and protect children'.

- The Knowledge and Skills Statement (DfE, 2015) for adults states that social workers 'should be able to communicate clearly, sensitively and effectively, applying a range of best evidence-based methods'.
- The HCPC Standards of Proficiency (2017) states that social workers should 'be able to engage in evidence-informed practice, evaluate practice systematically and participate in audit procedures'.

Practice wisdom

The notion of practice wisdom is particularly slippery in the social work literature as it has been defined in several ways. O'Sullivan (2005) highlights this in his description of practice wisdom while acknowledging its critiques, but in advocating for its value. As such, and with a sense of irony, O'Sullivan (2005: 222) draws attention to the binary way in which practice wisdom is described in the literature: practice wisdom is 'unreliable, personal, idiosyncratic knowledge built up through practice experience; and practice wisdom [is] the ability to make sound judgements in difficult, complex and uncertain situations'.

Rogers et al.'s (2016: 85) position aligns with the latter view proposing a positive stance to practice wisdom. They describe practice wisdom as holding potential for bridging the widely recognised gap that exists in terms of theory/knowledge and daily practice: 'Practice wisdom is the foundation for effective practice. It encompasses both the art and science of social work, and so bridges the gap between theory and practice.'

In this claim, Rogers et al. argue that the 'art' of social work practice incorporates the creative, adaptable elements of practice with tacit knowledge, as well as the 'science' which refers to the aspect of practice using research, the evidence base and formal theory (Samson, 2015). As such, practice wisdom is not just a one-dimensional concept, but an amalgamation of knowledge forms brought into effect in the practice context.

Some authors illuminate the co-productive nature of practice wisdom in that it evolves from the relationship and interaction between a social worker and people in receipt of support. As such, it is participatory, collaborative and socially constructed (Litchfield, 1999).

> ### Danger point: neither reflective nor reflexive practice
>
> While the different conceptualisations of practice wisdom offer an illustration of how social workers can competently draw together a range of forms of knowledge to inform their practice, there is a danger that experienced practitioners might then lose the ability to be critically reflective, reaching the point where they consider their practice wisdom to be complete and their practice akin to that of an 'expert'. This is never the case as the need for dynamic, reflexive practice never disappears as the social world continually evolves and people's unique social circumstances constantly change. Therefore, practice wisdom does not equate to 'expert' practice but to skilled and adaptable use of ever-evolving bodies of knowledge.

Moreover, this means that practice wisdom is gained and developed through experience. It is, therefore, not static (it does not remain the same) but dynamic (it changes over time and in different spaces).

Evaluating forms of knowledge

Dunne (2011: 18) argued that 'professional judgement involves the ability to actuate knowledge with relevance, appropriateness, or sensitivity to the context', but it is also important to determine the quality of the knowledge that you use. In 2003 the Social Care Institute for Excellence (SCIE) undertook a pragmatic knowledge review in an attempt to create a classificatory and evaluation framework for social work. The knowledge review identified the main types of research, experience and wisdom that combine to form the social work knowledge base in use, including: policy; organisational; research; practitioner; and user knowledge. The research team proposed the TAPUPAS tool for evaluating these forms of knowledge. Applying the TAPUPAS framework enables you to appraise the quality of sources of knowledge. Pawson et al. (2003: ix) concluded that knowledge should be tested for:

- **T**ransparency – are the reasons for it clear?
- **A**ccuracy – is it honestly based on relevant evidence?
- **P**urposivity – is the method used suitable for the aims of the work?
- **U**tility – does it provide answers to the questions it set?
- **P**ropriety – is it legal and ethical?
- **A**ccessibility – can you understand it?
- **S**pecificity – does it meet the quality standards already used for this type of knowledge?

Each standard can assist in the determination of status, in terms of quality and value, given to a knowledge claim within a specific context, and in providing criteria by which knowledge claims are judged the TAPUPAS framework reminds us to use knowledge critically and reflectively.

Rutter and Brown (2015) offer a different way to think about assessing *new* knowledge in practice. Their framework (see Table 2.3) is based on an inductive approach where reasoning is developed first). As argued by Rutter and Brown, using a framework to assess knowledge in this way offers a robust and systematic model (rather than a ad hoc or trial-and-error approach) and will enable you to 'demonstrate, evidence and evaluate the type of learning achieved' (Rutter and Brown, 2015: 27). This will require conscious and thoughtful deliberation and might not implicitly include less tangible aspects of an assessment (such as your emotions and interpretation), but this is not to say that these should be discounted. You should also consult Chapter 3 on critical reading for more appraisal frameworks.

Table 2.3 Assessing new knowledge

Activities associated with using new knowledge in practice	Generic assessment criteria
A. Understand the situation's circumstances and needs, and your aims and objectives	Analysis, comprehension
B. Identify and evaluate relevant formal knowledge in respect of the above	Critical appraisal, evaluation
C. Combine principles with other knowledge, experience, ideas and values	Transformation of abstract data and concepts, synthesis
D. Use to inform or direct decisions and actions	Design, creativity, transfer
E. Critically monitor and judge decisions and actions	Evaluation

Source: Rutter and Brown (2015: 28)

SUMMARY

In this chapter we have introduced you to lots of information about 'knowledge'. By starting with an overview of the links between knowledge, epistemology and ontology, we have introduced you to some key terminology and concepts in the philosophy of knowledge. This is quite complex, but it is important that as you develop your skills you have a foundational understanding of the philosophical underpinnings of critical thinking. We have also included some questions about 'what counts as knowledge' by exploring different forms of knowledge (some in greater depth). This will give you an essential foundation in terms of the different forms of knowledge available to you in practice contexts. You should, however, always use different forms of knowledge with a critical lens. That is, make sure that you question the source of knowledge, that you query whether that knowledge can be verifiable and that you ask yourself whether it is appropriate to apply this knowledge in the circumstances.

In addition, you have considered the different avenues of social work discourse in recent times in terms of what is the best type of knowledge to use to support your practice decisions. There is a significant amount of literature debating evidence-based practice and evidence-informed practice, and further reading will help you to decipher the different ways in which you can approach this topic including using EBP in your own work. Again, you will need to read widely while noting the limitations of any approach or evidence. This is particularly the case if you find yourself in more formal practice settings (such as a court) where you can be asked to justify your decision-making and comment on the credibility of your evidence. In conclusion, you have a wealth of knowledge to collect during the social work task of completing assessments, planning and intervening and should strive to use the best approach for each unique situation.

Having read this chapter, you should be able to:

- Understand the link between philosophy and knowledge production
- Identify a range of forms of knowledge from that offered by experts by experience ('user and carer knowledge') to research and theoretical knowledge
- Use a critical lens and identify both advantages and disadvantages of using different forms of knowledge in social work practice
- Consider the value of evidenced-informed practice and practice wisdom as different forms of knowledge and approaches to practice.

FURTHER READING

Beresford, P. (2000). Service users' knowledge and social work theory: Conflict or corroboration? *British Journal of Social Work*, 30(4), 489–503.

Mathews, I. and Crawford, K. (2011). *Evidence-Based Practice in Social Work*. Exeter: Learning Matters.

Trevithick, P. (2012). *Social Work Skills and Knowledge: A Practice Handbook* (3rd edn). Maidenhead: McGraw-Hill Education.

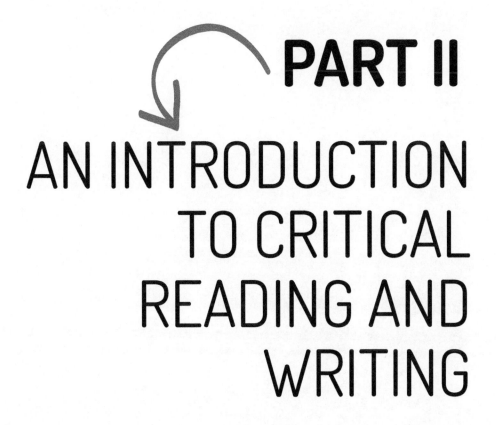

PART II

AN INTRODUCTION TO CRITICAL READING AND WRITING

3

CRITICAL READING

THEORETICAL BACKGROUND

- Learning outcomes and QAA/HCPC
- Benchmark and verification of knowledge
- Critical reflection and reflexivity
- Applying critical thinking
- Evidencing, evaluating and synthesising knowledge

RELEVANCE TO SOCIAL WORK THINKING AND PRACTICE

- Identification, appraisal and verification of knowledge
- Analysis
- General knowledge

REAL-WORLD CHALLENGES

- Lack of or limited research and searching skills
- Lack of record-keeping skills
- Low confidence in appraising and synthesising different ideas and perspectives
- Different learning styles
- Inaccessibility of technical empirical research
- Reluctance to read

Introduction

To develop the skills required to embed critical thinking in social work education and within the praxis of social work, this chapter will highlight the importance of critical reading. We will explore the importance of adopting a critical orientation towards the recommendations advanced by theoretical and empirical knowledge found within social work literature. There are different ways to 'read', but reading for a university course is fundamental to successful studies. This chapter will illustrate the importance of critical reading. It is, however, a skill that can be learnt and honed. It requires a more strategic approach than everyday reading for enjoyment as you need to have a clear reason and direction (that is, know why you are reading something) as well as a good sense of how to extract and evaluate relevant information.

Some of the chapters in this book contain a lot of theoretical and conceptual information, while the content of this chapter is much more practical. This is because, as lecturers in social work, we have learnt not to assume that students are experienced, avid readers. In actuality, reading for university can be a rather scary undertaking as expectations about what to read, how much to read and how to critically read are unclear. In this chapter we will help you to understand how academic reading skills can be learnt and the importance of developing a reading strategy early in your studies. Being able to read and extract key information is just the start. You will also need to be able to employ note-taking techniques that are aligned to the ways in which you work; just as we are all unique, not all note-taking techniques will be suitable for everyone. But it is not enough to read and take notes; you will also need to learn to appraise and synthesise key information. Reading for your studies is not as straightforward as first it seems! This chapter will provide lots of practical guidance and tips to enable you to develop critical reading skills.

 **Box 3.1   Activity**

Understanding your learner style (adapted from Honey and Mumford, 1982)

Having self-awareness is important for success on your learning journey, and knowing what type of learner you are is key from the start. Being able to adapt your reading approach to your learning style will help you to develop a reading strategy that is tailored to your specific learning style. Whichever type you are will influence the way in which you approach studying. This will influence the approach that you take to reading. For activists, engaging in periods of reading long pieces of text might prove to be more challenging, therefore we would advise doing this in 'chunks' (short bursts of reading). While pragmatists may prefer the practice of social work, reading for 'a better way' might be fruitful and the challenge lies in finding the model or theory.

Go to Appendix 1 (p. 173) and complete the Learning Styles Questionnaire and then work out which type of learner you are. There are four main types.

Activists involve themselves fully and without bias in new experiences. They enjoy the here and now and are happy to be dominated by immediate experiences. They are open-minded, not sceptical, and this tends to make them enthusiastic about anything new. Their philosophy is 'I'll try anything once'. They tend to act first and consider the consequences afterwards. Their days are filled with activity. They tackle problems by brainstorming. As soon as the excitement from one activity has died down they are busy looking for the next. They tend to thrive on the challenge of new experiences but are bored with implementation and longer-term consolidation. They are gregarious people constantly involving themselves with others, but in doing so they seek to centre all activities on themselves.

Reflectors like to stand back to ponder experiences and observe them from many different perspectives. They collect information, both at first hand and from others, and prefer to think about it thoroughly before coming to any conclusion. The thorough collection and analysis of data about experiences and events is what counts, so they tend to postpone reaching definitive conclusions for as long as possible. Their philosophy is to be cautious. They are thoughtful people who like to consider all possible angles and implications before making a move. They prefer to take a back seat in meetings and discussions. They enjoy observing other people in action. They listen to others and get the drift of the discussion before making their own points. They tend to adopt a low profile and have a slightly distant, tolerant unruffled air about them. When they act it is part of a wide picture which includes the past as well as the present and others' observations as well as their own.

Theorists adapt and integrate observations into complex but logically sound theories. They think problems through in a vertical, step-by-step logical way. They assimilate disparate facts into coherent theories. They tend to be perfectionists who will not rest easy until things are tidy and fit into a rational scheme. They like to analyse and synthesise. They are keen on basic assumptions, principles, theories models and systems thinking. Their philosophy prizes rationality and logic: 'If it's logical it's good'. Questions they frequently ask are: 'Does it make sense?', 'How does this fit with that?', 'What are the basic assumptions?' They tend to be detached, analytical and dedicated to rational **objectivity** rather than anything subjective or ambiguous. Their approach to problems is consistently logical. This is their 'mental set' and they rigidly reject anything that does not fit with it. They prefer to maximise certainty and feel uncomfortable with subjective judgements, lateral thinking and anything flippant.

Pragmatists are keen on trying out ideas, theories and techniques to see if they work in practice. They positively search out new ideas and take the first opportunity to experiment with applications. They are the sort of people who return from management courses brimming with new ideas that they want to try out in practice. They like to get on with things and act quickly and confidently on ideas that attract them. They tend to be impatient with ruminating and open-ended discussions. They are essentially practical, down-to-earth people who like making practical decisions and solving problems. They respond to problems and opportunities 'as a challenge'. Their philosophy is 'There is always a better way' and 'if it works it's good'.

Reading strategy

At the start of your studies, you might want to read textbooks which are at a basic level as they simply introduce you to social work concepts, theories, models, practice contexts and relevant legal frameworks. By the end of your course, you are likely to be more inclined to source texts that are in-depth and detailed and, more importantly, you should be accessing journal articles which report empirical research findings and contemporary theory. Those journal articles enable you to engage with and apply critical analysis to your academic work, and we keenly encourage you to use journal articles from the start of your studies. This will enable you to achieve depth and critique in your **synthesis** and analysis which will be reflected in your written work. This is critical thinking in action!

The amount that you need to read might take you by surprise at the start of your course; it will be more than you are prepared for, but it will make a radical difference to your learning if you read both strategically and widely from the start. To get the most out of your studies it is important that you embed a reading strategy from the outset, with time set aside to read before and after taught sessions; this will wholly enhance your ability to understand the taught content of the course and develop key skills such as the ability to apply theory to real-world contexts. This is particularly important if you are new to studying social sciences. It is often more beneficial to read different authors on the same topic, as this helps your understanding too. All this requires time. Every module and course will have a reading list, so familiarise yourself with this at the start of the module and try to devise a reading strategy that aligns with the content of the module and the order in which it is taught. In addition, every module, course or planned session will have learning outcomes and specified readings, and you should align your reading choices with these. This may be in addition to the recommended reading.

Practical considerations: time and space

Some of you might be continuing your studies from an undergraduate degree in a different subject, while some of you might be returning to study (at either undergraduate or postgraduate level) after a significant break. Therefore, we thought that it would be helpful to remind you of some practical considerations and that your reading strategy needs to embed the requirements of the module and course more generally, but it also needs to incorporate your personal life demands. For example, if you have children and they are at school, it might be that every Thursday and Friday, when you have no scheduled teaching, your study time begins at 10 am and finishes at 2 pm to fit in with the school run. However, you might work on a part-time basis alongside your studies and it might be impossible to set time aside to study during the daytime. Every Sunday might be your study day. If so, you should set your alarm clock and treat it as a work day. Have breakfast, take a cup of tea or bottle of water and begin at 9 am. Take your breaks and clock off at 4 pm. You will be surprised at how much you can achieve in a dedicated day of independent study.

If you are short for time as you have competing demands, then you need to have an efficient approach to reading, and time spent thinking about how you are going to schedule your study time will pay off in the long term. In order to use any spare time effectively, you might wish to consult your tutor to ask if there is essential reading (and that which would be useful but can be skipped if you do not have the time). In this scenario, your reading strategy needs to prioritise quality over quantity.

Reading techniques

Fast-reading techniques: scanning and skimming

Employing fast-reading techniques can help you when you are short of time and need to ensure that what you study is relevant and essential. They also help when you have a large volume of work to get through, or if you have sourced a lot of material but only superficially picked it for relevance and need to scan through in order to be more discerning and select and reject texts. There are two approaches that are considered to be fast-reading techniques: scanning and skimming.

Scanning

This technique can be very helpful when you wish to find very specific information from a text without the need to closely read the whole text. This is a skilled activity in which you read quickly scanning for keywords or terms (see Box 3.2). It means that you do not need to read the entire text and therefore you can avoid reading content that is not relevant to your needs.

> ### Danger point: reading
>
> #### Concentration loss and drift
>
> Most people can only concentrate for short chunks of time (15–20 minutes in one go). So, if you do work for longer periods of time, you should try to do short blocks of reading and complete other study tasks in-between. You can entwine reading with different activities such as taking part in relevant e-learning which embeds reading, videos and activities (visit SCIE's website for an invaluable range of e-earning modules).
>
> #### Interruptions
>
> If you work at home and do not live alone, there is a danger of interruptions which can result in a loss of focus and concentration. Therefore, the time and place are both important in terms of your reading strategy. If the family are home on Sundays, it might be better to spend your independent study time at your university or the local library. Not everyone will have a dedicated study space at home.

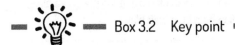 **Box 3.2   Key point**

Scanning for keywords

Blah blah blah READ QUICKLY TO blah blah blah blah blah blah blah blah blah blah blah blah blah blah blah blah blah blah blah blah blah blah blah blah blah blah blah blah blah blah blah

(Continued)

(Continued)

blah blah blah blah blah blah blah blah blah blah blah blah blah blah blah blah blah blah blah blah blah blah blah blah blah blah blah blah blah blah blah FIND THE IMPORTANT blah blah blah blah blah blah blah blah blah blah blah blah blah blah blah blah blah blah blah blah blah blah blah blah blah blah blah blah blah blah blah blah blah blah blah blah blah blah blah blah blah blah POINTS OR ARGUMENTS blah blah blah blah blah blah blah blah blah blah blah blah blah blah blah blah blah blah blah blah blah blah blah blah blah blah blah blah blah blah blah blah blah blah blah blah blah blah blah blah blah blah blah blah blah blah blah blah

Skimming

Another useful technique is skimming, which involves reading the text quickly to extract the main arguments in the text. You might not get a comprehensive and in-depth understanding of the topic, but you will get a feel for the main points (see Box 3.3). You can quite easily scan and skim at the same time. These are useful techniques when you have a lot of material to get through and you are looking for something in particular, or when you need to get started with researching a topic for an assignment. If you have a book chapter or journal article, use these techniques for reading the introduction and conclusion to get a quick feel for the text and in order to make a judgement about its value to you.

 Box 3.3　Key point

Skimming for main points

Blah blah blah READ THE KEY WORDS blah blah blah blah blah blah blah blah blah blah blah blah blah blah blah blah blah blah blah blah blah blah blah blah blah blah blah blah blah blah blah blah blah blah blah blah blah blah blah blah blah blah blah blah blah blah blah blah blah blah blah blah TO GAIN A SENSE OF THE ARGUMENT blah blah blah blah blah blah blah blah blah blah blah blah blah blah blah blah blah blah blah blah blah blah blah blah blah blah blah blah blah blah blah blah blah blah blah blah blah blah blah AND THE CONCLUSIONS BEING MADE blah blah blah blah blah blah blah blah blah blah blah blah blah blah blah blah blah blah blah blah blah blah blah blah blah blah blah blah blah blah blah blah blah blah blah blah blah blah blah blah

Good practice in making reading choices

Scanning and skimming techniques can help you to select learning resources and readings that are relevant, discarding those that are not. With textbooks and journal articles, this task can be relatively straightforward. However, with online resources, the world opens up to a huge range of possibilities for helping your learning along. That said, bear in mind that not all sources are credible (trustworthy). For example, newspaper articles that cite research, but do not state the source of this research, are not credible, and web pages that are sponsored by particular organisations (that have a business interest) may not be trustworthy. Try the activity in Box 3.4 to see if you are able to distinguish the credible from the not so credible learning resources.

Box 3.4   Activity

Learning resources

Read through the following list and decide if there are any resources that are not credible and that should not be used in your academic work:

1. Ahmed, A. and Rogers, M. (2016) *Working with Marginalised Groups: From Policy to Practice*. Basingstoke: Palgrave Macmillan.
2. The Equality Act 2010. https://en.wikipedia.org/wiki/Equality_Act_2010
3. Bowlby, J. (1969) *Attachment and Loss (Volume 1)*. London: Pimlico Books.
4. Gupta, A., Featherstone, B. and White, S. (2016) Reclaiming humanity: From capacities to capabilities in understanding parenting in adversity. *British Journal of Social Work*, 46(2), 339–354.
5. Joseph Rowntree Foundation (2018) *House to Home: Giving Social Housing Tenants a Place to Call Home*. London: JRF.
6. Social Work University Courses. https://www.thestudentroom.co.uk/forumdisplay.php?f=639
7. McKendrick, D. and Webb, S. (2014) Taking a political stance in social work. *Critical and Radical Social Work*, 2(3), 357–369.
8. Rogers, M., Whitaker, D., Edmondson, D. and Peach, D. (2016) *Developing Skills for Social Work Practice*. London: Sage.

There are two sources in this list that are not credible; did you spot them? In the list, there are social work textbooks (1, 3 and 8), journal articles that are published in peer-reviewed academic journals (4 and 7) and a research report which is 'grey literature' (5). **Grey literature** is research which is either unpublished or published in a non-commercial form; for example, charity or government reports, policy statements or guidance or conference papers. You should not cite Wikipedia nor use chatrooms and other forums in your academic work unless there is a good reason for doing so, as these are not accepted to be credible sources. In choosing sources for academic studies, look for:

- Academic books – this includes edited collections, monographs (which offer an in-depth analysis of a topic), subject-specific reference books (such as social work dictionaries) and textbooks which can range from introductory texts to providing an overview of a theme (child protection, for example), the discipline (social work), an area of skill (communication, effective interviewing) or a particular group (asylum seekers and refugees, young carers).
- Journal articles – found in peer-reviewed journals. Articles can offer up-to-date empirical evidence on a subject (by reporting on a research study), explore contemporary issues (discussion papers) or provide an analysis and summary of the key literature on an issue (systematic literature reviews).
- Grey literature – government departments, quangos (non-governmental public bodies) and some of the major charities (NSPCC, Joseph Rowntree Foundation) publish very useful research reports.

Critical reading

Whether you are studying for an undergraduate or postgraduate qualification in social work, there will be an expectation for you to use critical thinking skills in all aspects of your studies and practice. Critical thinking skills are integral in reading for your studies. You will be introduced to, and will come across in your independent study, a range of material from different sources and you should approach all of it with a critical lens. This means being able to scrutinise and evaluate different sources of knowledge (theory, legislation, research and practice knowledge; see Chapter 2 for a discussion of critical knowledge) presented by different authors. You will need to be able to recognise objectivity and **subjectivity** in different knowledge as it is presented in the written word. These are two important philosophical concepts: objectivity is the quality or position of being neutral, and without bias or prejudice, whereas subjectivity is the quality or position of being based on or influenced by personal feelings, tastes, opinions or experiences. Being a critical reader requires you to recognise objectivity and subjectivity in written forms, but also it demands a reflective stance (see Chapter 5) and the ability to identify your own objective or subjective responses to the content of your chosen reading. As such, you should now be able to see how being a critical reader is not about being negative. In academic terms, being critical means being able to critique, taking an objective stance and looking at texts and asking questions (see Chapter 1).

Reading journal articles

It is imperative from the start of your studies, whether you are an undergraduate or postgraduate student, that you access, read and critique journal articles. This type of reading enables you to engage with up-to-date theorising and the research evidence on any given topic. Reading journal articles enables you to consider the value of contemporary thought or research and how this enables the development of theory, practice or policy. Reading and using journal articles in your academic work will enable you

 Box 3.5   Key point ■■■■■■■■■■■■■■■■■■■■■■■■■■■

Critical questions for reading

Table 3.1

Author perspectives	Who is the author and what is their perspective or paradigm (worldview)? Is there an alternative view offered? Is there a conclusion, and, if so, does the author make clear and reasonable conclusions?
Analysis and critique	Is the argument clear or is the author making claims which are unsupported, or contested by other authors that you have read?
Objective or subjective	Are there implicit/explicit value judgements? Does the author make generalisations that are unreasonable or biased? Has the work cited been supported by an organisation that might have influenced any reported outcomes (e.g. in providing funding for the research findings that are presented)?
Evidence-based	What is based on evidence and what is an opinion? Are there unfounded assumptions? Does the author draw on evidence that is traceable and reliable? Are there 'clear and reasonable conclusions' founded on the evidence?
Relevance	Does the author make claims that do not seem to be supported by the findings of the research that they cite or that are pertinent to the rest of the discussion?
Thoroughness	Can you identify any clear omissions, errors or gaps?
Quality and provenance	Is the research that the author is basing their main points on credible/contemporary/relevant? Does the author utilise sources that are not credible (e.g. web-based sources that are not scientific or systematic)?
Method	If the author is reporting research, are the methods evident, and is the analysis presented with clarity?

to embed a more critical discussion using up-to-the-minute evidence and knowledge, whereas if you rely upon academic textbooks, the likelihood is that you will produce a rather descriptive account of the topic.

You can use critical questions more systematically when reading peer-reviewed journal articles, and there are various tools that are freely available and can guide you through this (see the Critical Appraisal Skills Programme at https://casp-uk.net/). An appraisal tool is usually targeted towards journal articles which report particular types of research:

- **Qualitative research** – an approach to researching the social world which focuses on language (rather than numbers and the quantification of data). Qualitative research seeks to interpret meanings and provide insights into social life. Qualitative research focuses on subjective experiences.
- **Quantitative research** – usually emphasises quantification in the collection and analysis of data. As a research strategy it incorporates a natural science model of the research process and is more concerned with objectivity and fact.

- **Mixed methods research** – research that combines methods associated with both quantitative and qualitative approaches.
- **Systematic reviews** – a methodology that systematically reviews the current evidence (literature) on a particular issue. It is a comprehensive and transparent approach to reviewing literature which is capable of replication. (Bryman, 2015)

Appraisal tools can be useful as prompts for the critical reading of research-based journal articles. These ask questions focusing on key sections of a paper, for example:

- Title – is this appropriate and clear (that is, does it reflect the content of the paper)?
- Abstract – is it explicit and representative of the paper?
- Introduction – does it provide a rationale and set the scene? That is, is the purpose and reason for the paper made clear and justified? Do you identify any errors of fact and representation (that is, has the author misinterpreted existing theory or the research of others)? The issue of misrepresentation is something that will be evident to you if you have read widely around the topic.
- Methodology – are the study design and method for data collection suitable in relation to the research question (is the research questions explicitly stated)? Is the sampling strategy evident, and is the sample of a reasonable size? How were participants recruited? Is the data analysis strategy clearly stated and justified? Did the researchers obtain ethical approval? Are any sensitive issues addressed? Could you replicate the study from the methodology description?
- Findings and discussion – are the findings clearly presented? Does the author make claims that are not supported by the findings? Is the discussion relevant? Does the author use the findings and link to any relevant existing literature or current knowledge? Are the findings overstated in terms of what they add to current thinking, or does the author not state their importance enough?
- Implications – are recommendations for practice or policy made, and are these justified in light of the study's findings?

Danger point: understanding complex material

First tip: don't panic! Not all academic literature is written in an accessible way; it may be that sourcing another author who writes on the same subject will prove fruitful and enable you to understand complex concepts. Alternatively, you may have been tasked with reading a more complex piece for an assessed piece of work, or preparatory work for a teaching session. There are ways to approach more complex material:

- Read it once, then take a break. Read it again more slowly and take time thinking about what the author is saying.
- Use the stop–review technique (The Open University, 2007) where you read a couple of paragraphs then stop and write notes. Even if you are struggling to understand the argument that the author is making, putting this into your own words can help you to work out the author's meaning or perspective.
- Have an online dictionary and thesaurus open on your laptop or phone. When you come across complex sentences or words, use the dictionary to understand a word, and use the thesaurus to look for synonyms that might be more familiar to you.
- Try to write the author's point in your own words.
- If you are reading about a particular social work theory or model, use Google to find introductory online guides (but do not cite in your own work unless you find a credible source – not Wikipedia!).

The SQ3R reading technique

The SQ3R technique (Robinson, 1970) can make your reading strategy more efficient and productive, saving time and enabling a better understanding of the material. Box 3.6 explains the acronym and the approach; it serves as a reminder for careful and critical reading.

 Box 3.6 Key point

The SQ3R reading technique

Survey – Survey the text to extract the general meaning or idea. Use scanning or skimming to get the 'gist' and a quick overview. Read the introduction and conclusion to get a feel for what is discussed and presented.

Question – Think about the questions that you would like the text to answer. Think about what you know and what you don't know. Think what is it you need to know.

Read – Read carefully if you think the text is relevant and useful. Don't get sidetracked!

Recall – Recall the main points (hence read carefully).

Review – Review the text to confirm that you have extracted and correctly remembered all the main points that are useful for your work.

Then... *critique*! Thinking about the points that you extracted from the text, can you critique the position taken, or think of other readings that offer an alternative view? Does the author use evidence to verify claims made, or are there claims that go unsubstantiated? Are there gaps? And so on. Always try to return to a critical line of questioning.

Danger point: neglecting the 'expert by experience'

It is vitally important when you are reading for your studies that you ask questions of the text (whether it is a book, journal article or research report). More fundamentally, however, it is important to consider whether the text authentically or respectfully reflects the lived experience of service users. In other words, does the knowledge that is portrayed in the text reflect a particular, often one-dimensional, view (that is, of the researcher or the profession), and how accurate is that view in terms of the perspectives or experiences of the people that we work with? We can use the term 'expert by experience' to acknowledge the position that service users are experts on their own lives when seeking to evaluate knowledge and its application to practice scenarios. For instance, if you are reading a research report that was produced by a government agency (say, the Department of Health) about the social care needs of people affected by dementia, consider who funded that piece of work, and what agenda they start with. Will this influence the outcomes of the research project and will it influence the way in which the findings of the project are presented in that report? The answer is, yes! The key question is, does the report reflect the needs and experiences of service users, people who live with dementia or who care for someone with dementia, and who are 'experts by experience'?

 Box 3.7 Activity

Applying criticality in reading

Read through the following paragraph. This is the abstract (or summary) for a journal article. Use your critical and analytical skills to draw out any issues or weaknesses with this abstract. The sentences are numbered and linked to our comments in Appendix 2 (p. 185).

Developing a strengths-based response to victims of domestic abuse

Abstract:

(1) This article presents the findings of a study that was conducted with social workers, employed in child protection services, in terms of their views about practice in the context of domestic abuse. (2) Domestic abuse is a well known social problem which affects everybody. (3) Statistics suggest that 1 in 4 women will experience domestic abuse and 1 in 10 children up to the age of 16 will have lived with domestic abuse in their family context. (4) Therefore, it is evident that it is a significant issue affecting a whole range of people who encounter child protection services. (5) It's clear that most women will experience domestic abuse and it is a gendered issue. (6) As such, it is an important issue for social work. (7) Due to its widespread recognition as a social problem, it is obvious that domestic abuse is one of the main issues for social work and subsequently, social work is informed by a strengths-based response. (8) A strengths-based response looks at people's unique abilities and coping strategies, rather than focusing on their deficits. (9) This research undertook dialogue with social workers in a focus group to uncover how this strengths-based practice was delivered in everyday practice contexts. (10) Findings verified that child protection social work takes a strengths-based response to families affected by domestic abuse and this offers the gold standard in terms of practice approaches.

....
....
....
....
....
....
....
....
....

Develop good habits: taking notes

Assembling meaningful and useful notes is a key skill. It is imperative to successful learning that you develop this early on in your studies. This helps to ensure that reading is productive and focused. Reading is often task-driven when linked to your studies; that is, you are reading for a purpose. Part of the challenge is moving from one subject to another, and in taking good notes when teaching styles vary from one lecturer to another. Once you have become accustomed to a lecture or teaching style, it is easier to glean the important points to make note of (rather than writing everything down; particularly with lecturers who meander or tell long stories, which makes it a little more challenging to extract the most pertinent information). One of the important things for you to understand here is that this is a skill that you can then transfer to practice. When visiting service users in their homes, they will not necessarily tell you a linear or brief story about their particular situation or problem. Extracting key information and making clear, succinct notes about what is relevant to your social work assessment is essential.

Note-taking and active listening

Active listening helps you to be aware of how you are communicating, while observing and listening to others and while remaining conscious of your internal voice as it responds to the communication of others; this is a demanding task (Rogers et al., 2016). It is a useful skill to hone in the classroom as it provides you with the ability to engage in a reflective listening mode, drawing out information that is important, discarding information that is irrelevant and considering your own responses. This is the same skill that you will be encouraged to develop in the real world of practice when with service users, carers or professionals. Fundamentally, the task involves gathering information (from your lecturer), synthesis, analysis and critical thinking.

There are strategies that you can adopt if you worry about concentration. Be alert for summaries and listen out for clues in your lecturer's speech such as vocal emphasis, or the use of words and phrases such as 'however' and 'on the other hand'. This is where your lecturer is giving you contrasting perspectives (essential in developing a critical analysis). Written materials (such as handouts and PowerPoint slides) can aid your memory, but your lecturer will often talk about the points on these in greater depth, and even add new important insights. Do not, therefore, rely on the provision of written aids. Try to listen to the answers to questions asked by your peers as these often help to clarify points being made (and often these are concepts or arguments that many people in the room are struggling to make sense of) and can give you some important pointers for alternative perspectives.

Good habits

Making useful notes that you can refer back to (and understand) will save you time and effort in the long run. This is especially the case if you get to Year 2 and want to find those notes on reading that would be useful now but you did it in the first semester in Year 1. See Box 3.8 for our top tips.

 Box 3.8 Key point

Top tips on note-taking

- Bear in mind the questions you are seeking to address or the topic that you are interested in and focus your reading and note-taking on these.
- Develop a system of colour coding (using different pens) if you are a visual learner (an activist). Highlighter pens and coloured sticky notes can all help you to develop a recording system. Alternatively, organise your notebook so that there are separate sections for different subjects.
- Use a mind map to capture the ideas contained within a text (see Figure 3.1).

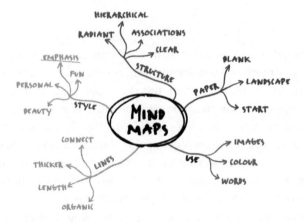

Figure 3.1 Mind mapping

- Keep a notebook for notes so that you keep all your notes together or use A–Z cards and develop a filing system. This is helpful if you struggle to remember definitions and key concepts. Have a card for each concept, theory or technical word with a definition that is written in your own words so that you can understand it, and refer to it when you encounter the concept, theory or technical word. This will help you to learn and remember these.
- Avoid copying long sections of text as this is a passive form of note-taking; that is, you do not learn from doing so. It also reflects a passive approach to reading, rather than active reading. Instead, try to paraphrase as the act of doing so helps you to engage with the information presented. You stand a better chance of internalising the meaning in this way.
- In addition to making notes and paraphrasing, add your own thoughts, interpretations or ideas about the subject. Perhaps a link to some other reading

if you can offer a similar or counter perspective that you have come across before.

- Another help when reading for study is to have your phone or a laptop handy and to have an online dictionary and thesaurus open and ready to help you with those tricky words or concepts. Keep a written record of these (in a dedicated notebook or those A–Z cards) and refer back to them as necessary.

- Do not forget to record the source of your reading with your notes. Include the author, book or journal title, page, the article title and whatever else is appropriate. Otherwise, you could return to your notes and not be able to remember that book or journal article. This is especially important if you are writing about a specific concept or theory as you will need to cite that reference or article to ensure that the reader is signposted to the source. Each university will have its own system of referencing; ensure that you familiarise yourself with this early on in your studies. Universities will offer online guides and most likely a quick guide; print this and use it!

- A similar and related point needs to be made about the use of direct quotes. If you find an excellent quote that really makes a point so well that you wish to include it in your written work then make sure that you include speech marks in your notes so that you know where the quote starts and ends and can reproduce it correctly in your work and attribute it to the author. These days all universities have plagiarism software, and if you do not accurately cite another person's work you can find yourself referred for academic malpractice.

- You might prefer to type notes, and it is imperative that you organise your computer files by setting up a folder structure with meaningful names. Perhaps use different modules that you study (Introduction to Professional Practice, Law for Social Work, Working with Adults) or set up by theme (law and social policy, communication skills, children and families social work; mental health, domestic abuse). A word of warning: if you do use your laptop or a USB stick, remember to back up your work on a regular basis.

Some techniques are introduced above, but there are many different methods that might work for you, and these include:

- Text-based notes – writing notes in your notebook, creating word documents, creating tables
- Visual methods – mind maps, systems mapping, colour coding, line diagrams
- Audio memos – using a computer, mobile phone or another digital recorder to make notes that you can listen to whenever you want.

Always remember that you may want to return to your notes for an essay, future module, or exam. Therefore, whatever system you develop should be useful, consistent and rigorous. Moreover, it should be reliable, so that when you return to it, your notes are legible and make sense! Use a technique that suits you.

■ ■ **Box 3.9   Activity** ━━━━━━━━━━━━━━━━━━━

Note-taking quiz

Which of the following is *not* a good strategy for preparing for a lecture?

a. Reading notes from the last session
b. Preparing terms or concepts that you are struggling to understand, to check out your understanding with the lecturer
c. Doing any preparatory reading and making notes
d. Asking your peers if the lecturer noticed you were absent from the last session.

What is *not* a 'top tip' for making good notes?

a. Put the ideas or arguments that you read into your own words
b. Highlight unfamiliar vocabulary or complex, unclear ideas
c. Develop a coding system or abbreviations in your note-taking
d. Don't write anything but your own thoughts on a subject.

When attending a teaching session, which of the following is *not* a useful clue to the key information that is being provided?

a. Lecturer's vocal emphasis
b. Words and phrases in bold on the slides or handouts
c. Summaries or recaps
d. Someone's notes.

If you chose 1 or more d) options. Read this chapter again!

SUMMARY

The art and technical aspects of critical reading mean that this is an activity that intrinsically underpins successful study and, as such, developing good habits and skills in critical reading is key from the start of your course. Reading well is something that can be developed with practice. It involves being methodological and organised, but also it means that you have to be engaged as a reader as this is an active, not passive, activity.

Having read this chapter, you should be able to:

- Consider the ways that academic reading requires a more active approach than everyday reading
- Value the importance of the 'expert by experience' when seeking to evaluate knowledge and its application to social work practice
- Confidently read a variety of literature with a critical eye
- Develop a usable strategy for note-taking.

FURTHER READING

Bottomley, J., Cartney, P. and Pryimachuk, S. (2018). *Studying for Your Social Work Degree*. St Albans: Critical Publishing.

Cottrell, S. (2017). *Critical Thinking Skills* (3rd edn). London: Macmillan International.

Stogdon, C. and Kiteley, R. (2010). *Study Skills for Social Workers*. London: Sage.

4

CRITICAL WRITING

THEORETICAL BACKGROUND

- Learning outcomes and QAA/HCPC
- Critical reflection to demonstrate deep and extensive learning
- Applying critical thinking
- Evidencing, evaluating and synthesising knowledge

RELEVANCE TO SOCIAL WORK THINKING AND PRACTICE

- Verification of knowledge
- Analysis
- General knowledge

REAL-WORLD CHALLENGES

- Limitation in assignment planning
- One-dimensional or limited perspectives
- Single underdeveloped views on socio-political challenges
- Limitations in assignment structured
- Lack of confidence in referencing and independent thought
- Low confidence in writing

Introduction

This chapter will help you to understand why academic writing is important within the context of studying social work. Writing is one of the main ways that you can demonstrate your knowledge, values and skills through the assessments that will be integrated throughout your university studies. We will help you to identify the differences between description and analysis within academic writing. As a foundation from which to grow and nurture the knowledge, values and skills needed in critical thinking, we will provide you with lots of examples of the writing techniques and tools to enhance your production of written assignments and practical advice about how to develop and embed analysis within a piece of academic writing. These examples will guide you through the common mistakes made by students in academic work and show, by example, how to improve through the critical application and substantiation of evidence in written assignments.

While reflective writing is an important component of social work education, this is explored elsewhere (see Chapter 5) and this chapter focuses on a more traditional academic assignment as it is likely that during your social work studies you will have to produce both types of written assignment. There are, however, some common features of these different types of assignment and these include applying theory, embedding critical analysis, using evidence to substantiate claims, and embedding good practice in terms of academic conventions (with consistent and accurate referencing, for example). We will cover the basics: planning and structuring your written work in order to illustrate the value of organising your work so as to build arguments throughout your critical discussion. First, it is important to engage in an exercise of self-reflection and consider what type of writer you are (see Box 4.1).

 ▬▬ Box 4.1 Activity ▬▬▬▬▬▬▬▬▬▬▬

What type of writer are you?

Before you consider the value of planning and structuring your work, it is helpful to reflect upon the way in which you approach writing tasks. Creme and Lea (1997) identified four types:

The *diver writer*. This person leaps straight in and starts the writing process early on, in order to find out what they want to say. There is not necessarily a plan as the diver starts anywhere to see what emerges, and may subsequently formulate a writing plan.

The *patchwork writer*. In the early stages of the process, this type of writer works on sections (perhaps using subheadings), and then combines each section later.

The *grand plan writer*. This type of writer will read and make notes before formulating a plan or beginning writing. They will have an almost complete picture of the written piece before they put pen to paper.

The *architect writer*. The architect is a planner and will produce a detailed plan, mind map or spider diagram early in the process. This will guide the work. They will, therefore, have a sense of the structure (perhaps even before the content).

Which most accurately depicts your approach to planning and writing?

Planning

An essential process must be undertaken in order to structure and organise your written work. You need to understand the assigned task. This might feel like stating the obvious, but it is not unusual for students to misinterpret assignment questions and guidance. You should begin by identifying the process words and the content words.

Process words offer an instruction. They tell you what you need to do. For example, '*compare* the approaches ...' or '*assess* the impact of ...'. See Table 4.1 for a comprehensive list of common process words and their meanings. In contrast to process words, *content words* indicate the topic or theme of an assignment. Content words are often nouns.

 ━━ Box 4.2   Activity ━━━━━━━━

Process and content words

Identify the process and content words in the following assignment task (the answer is given in Appendix 2, on p. 186):

> The Mental Capacity Act 2005 states that 'a person must be assumed to have capacity unless it is established that he lacks capacity'. Discuss the ethical challenges to social workers that may arise as a result of this principle.

....
....
....
....

Whenever you are given an assignment, use the process and content words to break down the assignment task, which will help to determine: what you need to do and how you will need to approach the topic; the specific focus of the discussion; or which aspects of the discussion will need to have greater importance.

Table 4.1 Common process words and their meaning

Process word	Definition
Account for	Explain something, or clarify.
Analyse	Identify the main points and significant features. Examine critically and/or in great detail.
Assess (see *evaluate*)	Identify the value of something. Weigh arguments for and against something, indicating and then assessing the strength of the evidence on both sides.
Compare	Show similarities between two (or more) things. Indicate relevance, importance and consequence of these similarities.
Contrast	Show differences between two (or more) things. Indicate relevance, importance and consequence of these differences. If appropriate, justify why one item/argument may be more convincing or preferred.
Compare and contrast	Show the similarities and differences between two (or more) things.
Criticise	Make a judgement based on evidence and reasoning, and using examples, about the merit of two or more related things; for example, theories, opinions, models.
Define	Provide the exact meaning of a word, concept or phrase. Where appropriate, you may need to problematise the definition, identify flaws and alternative definitions.
Demonstrate	Use examples to show something.
Describe	Outline the main characteristics or features of something, or how something works.
Discuss	Explain and give arguments for and against an issue; consider the implications of; then reach a conclusion. Often used in connection with a quotation or statement that can be disputed.
Distinguish or differentiate between	Look for differences between.
Evaluate (see *assess*)	Assess the worth, importance, validity, effectiveness of something using evidence. There will probably be a case both for and against. Be clear about your criteria for how you judge which side is preferable/more convincing.
Explain	Clearly identify why something happens or why it is the way that it is. Usually involves looking at evidence/arguments for and against and weighing them up.
Illustrate	Make clear, visible and explicit, usually requiring carefully chosen examples.
Interpret	Provide the meaning and relevance of something.
Justify	Provide evidence supporting an argument/point of view/idea. Show why a decision is made or conclusions are drawn, considering and exploring objections.
Outline	Identify the main features or points on a topic, omitting minor details and emphasising the main structure (see *summarise*).
Rationalise	Attempt to explain or justify something with logical, plausible reasons (even if not appropriate or correct).
Relate	Show similarities and connections between two or more things.
Summarise	Draw out the main points only (see *outline*).
To what extent	Consider how far something is true and how convincing the evidence is, including any ways in which the proposition remains unproven.

Gillett et al. (2009: 20) provide another useful summary of common words found in assignment titles or briefings. An adapted list is provided in Table 4.2.

Table 4.2 Common words in assignment guidance

Common words	Definition
Concept	An idea or a general notion
Concise	Short, brief
Context	The circumstances that form the setting for an event, idea or phenomenon, and in terms of which it can be understood and evaluated
Criteria	A principle or standard by which something may be judged or decided
Factor(s)	A circumstance, or influence, that contributes to an outcome or result
Function	The purpose of something
Implications	The consequence or conclusion of something (can be short- or long-term)
Limitations	A restriction, or limited circumstance of something
Significance	Meaning and importance
Validity	The quality of being logically or factually sound or important

Source: Adapted from Gillett et al. (2009: 20)

Learning outcomes

All the assessed work that you complete will be accompanied by a set of *learning outcomes* (LOs). The LOs underpin the task, and you will need to meet each outcome in your written work. Therefore, it is imperative that you address each LO. Box 4.3 provides an example. Box 4.4 illustrates how you can ensure that you address the LOs in your plan.

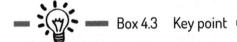 **Box 4.3 Key point**

Assignment tasks and learning outcomes

Module: Safeguarding and Law

Assignment task: The Mental Capacity Act 2005 states that 'a person must be assumed to have capacity unless it is established that he lacks capacity'. Discuss the ethical challenges to social workers that may arise as a result of this principle and apply theories of power and control.

Learning outcomes: In responding to the task, you will be required to demonstrate how you have met the following LOs:

1. Articulate how social work theories and concepts can assist our understanding of social work practice.

(Continued)

(Continued)

2. Critically evaluate the legal context of social work practice.
3. Demonstrate a critical understanding of diversity and difference in relation to ethical practice.

Structure

Depending on the type of writer that you are, you may or may not draw significantly on the planning stage to structure and organise your work. Whatever the discipline or assignment task, there is a common framework for structuring written work and this includes an introduction, a main body, and a conclusion. A good plan and structure will help to embed a coherent thread and result in a logical flow to the discussion. It will also help to organise your discussion so that a series of connected points or arguments result in building an argument or set of arguments keeping to the subject (and not meandering into unrelated territory). The three sections of a standard academic assignment (introduction, main body, conclusion) all serve a purpose and there are some general rules on what to include/omit and guidance on word lengths:

Introduction (10% of the word limit). The purpose of an introduction is to provide the reader with a sense of what will be addressed in the main discussion and why. You could start by incorporating the process words of the assigned task with, for example, 'This essay will explore …' or 'The purpose of this essay is to compare and contrast …'. You should include definitions of any key terms. You should indicate the structure and sequence of the main points in the discussion, but do so succinctly. The core perspectives or theoretical paradigms to be incorporated in your essay should be noted in the introduction, while leaving the detailed discussion for later.

Main body. Here you will present your main discussion.

Conclusion (10% of the word limit). This should provide a summary of your main points or arguments. Cottrell (2011: 186) notes that the conclusion should represent 'the inevitable end-point of your line of reasoning'. It is useful to give the reader a clear indication of where your conclusion begins, so you could use signal words such as 'In conclusion…' or 'In summary…'. Do not include new material here. You might summarise the main implications for practice.

 **Box 4.4   Key point**

Incorporating learning outcomes in your plan

Module: Safeguarding and Law

Assignment task: The Mental Capacity Act 2005 states that 'a person must be assumed to have capacity unless it is established that he lacks capacity'. Discuss the ethical challenges to social workers that may arise as a result of this principle and apply theories of power and control.

Learning outcomes: In responding to the task, you will be required to demonstrate how you have met the following LOs:

1. Articulate how social work theories and concepts can assist our understanding of social work practice.
2. Critically evaluate the legal context of social work practice.
3. Demonstrate a critical understanding of diversity and difference in relation to ethical practice.

The assignment:

Introduction. Let the reader know what you will be discussing in this essay and why. Define 'capacity' and indicate if this is the definition that you will use throughout your discussion.

Main body considerations. Construct a plan for each paragraph; you will need to have a main point or argument for each. For example, you could start with an evaluation of the Mental Capacity Act 2005 and how useful or restrictive it is in practice (LO 2). Explore how the Act can enhance/limit assessments and decision-making.

You will need to use theories of power and control in a critical analysis of the application of the Act in terms of the ethical challenges that can emerge; for example, the possibility of making decisions for a person that are not congruent with the views of that person or their family members, but which are in the person's best interests from a social work perspective (LOs 1 and 3).

You will need to ensure that you consider the issues of capacity, power and control in relation to a range of people with different backgrounds and characteristics (LO 3).

Explore the ways in which social workers (who are mostly female and White British) may apply the principles of the Act from a specific viewpoint (using their own experience of the world) but which might not be appropriate with families from minority groups. Include a critical analysis of cultural relativism (see Chapter 1) (LOs 1 and 3).

The main body will be broken down into several (perhaps five or six) main points (see Box 4.5). Each point should be explicitly relevant to the assignment task. In each paragraph, you should draw on evidence from research/experts by experience/theory/policy/ legislation/ other forms of knowledge to discuss and debate the ideas presented. Wherever possible, you should support the discussion with evidence (by citing and including references). So, if you cite a classic theorist or social work model, for example, **strengths-based** practice, you signpost the reader to the source (that is, you include a reference); unless, of course, you have constructed that theory or model and then quite rightly you should take credit for it! Using citations and referencing thoroughly demonstrates the authority and reliability of the evidence that you are using. It substantiates the claims that you are making and demonstrates how the argument is based upon a robust process of sourcing, selecting and appraising evidence to build your point or argument. The way that you use evidence is discussed further below.

Danger point: structure

Poor overall structure

A poor overall structure can lead to weak transitions (unrelated statements, or poor connections between paragraphs); disconnected and/or poorly framed arguments; repetition of points; and lack of a coherent, building an argument. A strong structure has related paragraphs, with a logical order. This is discussed in further detail below in the section on 'Organisation and Sequence'.

Poor paragraph structure

A sentence does not make a paragraph! Each paragraph should be 150–200 words in length. A paragraph should introduce a point or an argument, define any key terms, integrate smaller points that all relate to the main one, critically debate the main point or argument (that is, offer counter-perspectives), conclude the point or argument, and move to the next related point or argument in a new paragraph. This will demonstrate how you are able to evidence, evaluate and synthesise relevant knowledge.

Poor planning

Here are some ideas to get you started.

Subheadings. Type subheadings straight into a Word document, then use bullet points to make a few notes under each. Questions to ask yourself:

- Do all points make sense and belong under the subheading?
- Can you link each subheading, and are they all relevant?
- Can you link the last point under one subheading to the next subheading (to create a strong, logical transition)?

Mind maps. Create a mind map of ideas, as in Figure 4.1.

Reading and note-taking. Reading for an assignment while making detailed notes can help to start formulating and linking your ideas. Look through all your notes: are there some clear themes emerging?

Freewriting. Taking the content words, just start writing and see what happens! Ideas for the main body discussion are likely to start emerging from your thoughts. Remember that writing is a process and the final submission may be in its fifth, sixth or later version.

Reflection point. Review previous feedback on an earlier assignment. If you received comments about your organisation and structure, do they make sense within the context of this section? If not, reread this section and the next.

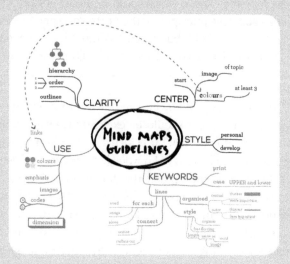

Figure 4.1   Mind map guidelines

Organisation and sequence

It is important to consider the order in which you present the arguments or points. You need to offer a critical discussion of each argument and ensure that there are explicit links between these. You need to sequence in such a way that you help the reader to understand the main argument that you are building and the perspective that you are taking. You should aim for a logical flow. You should aim to fully explore each argument or point, before moving to the next; do not return to the argument/point unless you are summarising in the concluding paragraph. If you do, you will create repetition which disrupts the flow of your discussion. A well-planned and well-ordered piece of work enables the reader to follow your train of thought as the main points stand out clearly and relate to one another. Signposting can be used ('as discussed earlier…') to direct a reader to a related point but you should not return to the arguments (unless, as noted, you are concluding).

Part of the skill of critical writing is being able to identify the most important aspects of your discussion and in knowing which need to go first in order to orient the reader to your line of inquiry or argument. If you sandwich the most important point between minor, inconsequential ones, then you run the risk of losing momentum, or of not being clear in terms of presenting the most important aspects of your discussion. In other words, your line of reasoning needs to be competently ordered or you run the risk of a disjointed discussion.

━ 🖉 ━ **Box 4.5　Activity** ━━━━━━━━━━━━━

Sequencing

Read these descriptions of a child protection conference: https://learning.nspcc. org.uk/child-protection-system/child-protection-definitions and http://www.safe guardingchildren.co.uk/child-protection-conferences.

Draft essay plan

Title: Critically discuss the current structure of the child protection conference.
　　Consider the following themes:

- Child, family and carer perspectives
- Conference chair role and remit
- Multi-agency partners
- Law and policy background
- Social worker role and remit

(Continued)

(Continued)

Think about the order that you might use and why.

Introduction: State what will be discussed in the main body and why. This should indicate the order of the topics included in the main body discussion, which should be logical and illustrate interconnections between each topic. We suggest the first theme to get you started.

Main body:

Theme 1: Law and policy background – this integrates a critical discussion of the definition, function and remit of a child protection conference to demonstrate an understanding of the legal and policy requirement for this process.

Theme 2 ....
....
....

Theme 3 ....
....
....

Theme 4 ....
....
....

Theme 5 ....
....
....

Conclusion: ....
....
....

Our suggestion can be found in Appendix 2 (p. 186).

Transitions

As noted above, good transitions (the connections between sentences or paragraphs) are important to creating a coherent, building argument. This is called signalling (Gillett et al., 2009). To do this, it is crucial to structure the information clearly and indicate exactly what you want to say by the use of signalling words. You will need to consider how you do this. Table 4.3 includes some signalling words that you can use within sentences, to connect sentences and to link paragraphs.

To ensure that one paragraph links to the next, use phrases such as 'Another aspect of …', 'A further perspective on …' or 'In contrast …'.

Table 4.3   Signalling words

Type of signalling words	Examples
Addition	In addition to, apart from this, as well as, furthermore, moreover, what is more, not only
Cause and effect	As a consequence, as a result, consequently, for this reason, hence, in order to, therefore, this leads to, thus
Comparison	In comparison, in the same vein, likewise, similarly
Condition	If, in that case, provided that, unless
Contrast/opposite ideas	Although, but, despite, in spite of, even so, however, in contrast, nevertheless, on the contrary, on the other hand, whereas, yet
Emphasis	Chiefly, especially, importantly, indeed, in detail, in particular, mainly, notably, particularly
Examples	For example, for instance, such as, thus, as follows
Explanation/equivalence	In other words, namely, or rather, this means, to be more precise
Generalisation	As a rule, for the most part, generally, in general, normally, on the whole, in most cases, usually
Summary/conclusion	Finally, in brief, in conclusion, in short, in summary, overall, to conclude
Support	Actually, as a matter of fact, in fact, indeed
Time/order	At first, eventually, finally, first(ly), in the first/second place, initially, lastly, later, next, prior to, second(ly)

Source: Gillett et al. (2009: 105)

The important thing to remember is not to let paragraphs stand alone, otherwise you cannot expect the reader to make the connection. You need to do this explicitly to demonstrate a logical line of reasoning.

Academic conventions: good habits to get into

What is meant by 'academic conventions'? These are the rules that apply to the majority of academic work. Many questions are linked to academic convention. For instance, do you need to produce a reference list? The answer is yes. A reference list is a list of all the references contained within your written assignment (this is discussed further below). Do you need to include definitions? Again, the answer is yes. In critical writing, it is required that when you include a theory/model/concept that might have various definitions, you include one to demonstrate to the audience which one you are utilising in your discussion, but include the others to illustrate the contested nature of the theory, models or concepts.

In academic writing, your ability to articulate your ideas and engage in contemporary debates is critical. Thus, your use of the English language is of vital importance and, again, there are academic conventions with which you should comply. For example, you should avoid jargon and acronyms, and, unless using direct quotes, you should avoid metaphors, as well as informal or colloquial language. For instance, rather than

'he stayed until the bitter end, but kind of wasn't aware that he was not wanted'

consider

'he stayed until the end, unaware that he was not welcome'.

Another rule of written English is that you should avoid contracted words; instead, write these in full. For instance, rather than 'didn't', 'couldn't' and 'isn't', you should write 'did not', 'could not' and 'is not'. The one exception is when you are including direct quotes.

Danger point: the passive voice

1. 'It has been reported that physical abuse is harmful'.
2. 'It has been argued that motivational interviewing is effective in cases of substance misuse'.
3. 'It was known that the children were neglected'.

Using the passive voice in these instances is not adequate in academic assignments (or other writing tasks for social work; for example, in report writing).
The basic sentence structure built upon the formula *subject–verb–object* is preferable. So, 'Dan told me' is more effective than 'I was told'. Using the passive voice leaves questions unanswered and accountability is lost. For example:

1. 'It has been reported that physical abuse is harmful'. Who has reported that? And harmful to whom and in what way?
2. 'It has been argued that motivational interviewing is effective in cases of substance misuse'. Who argues this?
3. 'It was known that the children were neglected'. It was known by whom?

In academic writing, there needs to be evidence for the claims that you make. So, in the case of example 2, you need to provide a citation (reference a source of that knowledge; for instance, a journal article) to provide the evidence or point the reader to work that illustrates that motivational interviewing is effective in cases of substance misuse:

Murphy (2018) has argued that motivational interviewing is effective in cases of substance misuse.

There are some other practices that you should adopt in relation to vocabulary and grammar. Specifically, think about your word choice. As well as the points made earlier about the passive voice and the need to avoid a conversational tone and metaphor, you should avoid making sweeping statements that are not supported by evidence. Use more tentative language. For example, rather than

'A holistic approach to risk assessments must be taken...'

consider

'A holistic approach to risk assessments should be taken....'

And rather than

'All social workers must adopt the policy...'

consider

'All social workers should consider the policy....'

So, avoid 'all', 'every', 'always', 'must', 'never'; instead use 'most', 'many', 'some', 'usually', 'in most cases', 'in few cases', 'it is unlikely that', 'suggests', 'it would appear'.

Academic conventions: objective versus subjective language

As noted earlier, there are two main types of social work essay: the traditional academic essay (discussed in this chapter) and the critical reflection. Another common question relating to academic essays is whether to use a first- or third-person narrative. This is not so straightforward in social work studies as it is more acceptable to use the first person (that is, make 'I' or 'my' statements), especially when writing reflectively (analysing personal or practice experiences). However, wherever possible academic conventions should be maintained, and this means using the third-person approach. Most academic writing is composed in the third person because it is more objective and less personal and subjective (see Chapter 3 for clarification on what is meant by objectivity and subjectivity). An example of third-person writing is 'this essay addresses …' rather than 'I will address …'.

Using objective language enables you to emphasise the information and arguments that you are presenting, rather than your personal opinions and views. For example, rather than

'I think that it is hard to use strengths-based practice in mental health social work.'

consider

'Data indicates that using strengths-based practice in mental health social work can be challenging'.

A more objective style requires evidence to substantiate your claims and indicates to the reader what you are reading and what you have learned. Compare the paragraphs in Box 4.6: which is the most objective and which presents the most convincing argument?

 Box 4.6 Key point

Objectivity versus subjectivity

Paragraph 1

Social workers have a responsibility to challenge social injustices and work with people facing adversity, but a tension can arise when they are tasked with providing support and services in times of a recession. For example, due to budget cuts and thinly spread resources, most local authorities have had to end funding for community provisions such as old people's day centres and children's Sure Start provision; prioritising instead safeguarding and those at highest risk. Therefore, while services are now provided within a neoliberal model, creating competition between providers and increasing choice and control for people who commission services, this is constrained by the availability in any given area when some services have been significantly affected by austerity and the withdrawal of funding and services.

Paragraph 2

Social workers must always challenge social injustices and help people faced with adversity. Why should the regular person in the street live with difficulties and not access the services that would help them to improve their lives when there are social workers in every local authority? And even though some services have disappeared because of austerity, why should I not be able to access a children's centre for my children when the person in the next county can? It is terribly unfair that services have been cut and people go without and this makes their problem worse.

Using more objective language also relies upon word choices that are not emotive. So, avoid words such as 'unfortunately', 'surprisingly' and 'thankfully'. Again, these tend to be used in more subjective ways and will indicate your personal opinion, rather than a perspective that is substantiated and supported with evidence. If you found paragraph 2 to be more subjective, then you were (of course) correct. Also, reflect upon the use of questions. Wherever possible, in academic essays you should avoid the use of questions to raise a point. This is not good academic practice.

Writing styles

The way in which you articulate yourself within a written assignment is central to demonstrating a range of skills including:

- critical thinking and evaluative skills;
- the ability to apply theory to real-world situations;

- the ability to synthesise different sources and forms of knowledge;
- the capacity to understand and articulate a balanced view by drawing from different perspectives;
- the ability to write for a particular audience.

One of the most important aspects of academic writing is the ability to develop a critical style. This does not come naturally to many and takes practise to hone.

Description versus analysis

One of the most common problems with academic assignments is the lack of critical analysis and the overly descriptive nature of the main body. Concentrating on including everything that you feel is relevant can lead to descriptive writing. It can obscure the main arguments and lack a central position where you offer a clear perspective. Whereas if you focus and choose a smaller number of arguments or points to be made, this will enable you to demonstrate a clear perspective and develop a more analytical, critical discussion. In this way, quality equals depth, and quantity can result in a descriptive, unfocused piece of writing. Remember that background information and history for context-setting are important but need to be kept to a minimum; include this type of descriptive detail where necessary.

Whenever you express a viewpoint or present an argument, you are making a claim that needs to be supported. You need to substantiate the claim by showing its validity. This is a good skill to develop early on your academic journey as it is also a skill that you will need as a social work practitioner; you cannot make claims that are unsubstantiated or unsustainable. Social workers need to be able to justify their decisions and sense-making processes. Students often struggle to differentiate between description and analysis at the start of their studies. Cottrell (2011) offers a succinct summary which helps to distinguish the two (see Table 4.4).

Table 4.4 Descriptive and critical analytical writing

Descriptive writing	Critical analytical writing
States what happened	Identifies the significance
States what something is like	Evaluates (judges the value of) strengths and weaknesses
Gives the story so far	Weighs one piece of information against another
States the order in which things happened	Makes reasoned judgements
Says how to do something	Argues a case according to the evidence
Explains what a theory says	Shows why something is relevant or suitable
Explains how something works	Indicates why something will work (best) and what its limitations are
Notes the method used	Indicates whether something is appropriate or suitable

(Continued)

Table 4.4 (Continued)

Descriptive writing	Critical analytical writing
Says when something has occurred	Identifies why the timing is of importance
States the different components	Weighs up the importance of component parts
States options	Gives reasons for selecting each option
Lists details	Evaluates the relative significance of details
Lists in any order	Structures information in order of importance
States links between items	Shows the relevance of links between pieces of information
Gives information	Draws conclusions

Source: Cottrell (2011: 232)

Consider the above description which delineates the approach to essay structures and paragraph planning. In this description, we argue that good practice in an essay structure involves planning so that each paragraph introduces an argument, defines key terms, develops a series of smaller points that relate to the main argument and then draws a conclusion (this is the end of the paragraph). Look at the example in Box 4.7.

― 🖎 ― **Box 4.7 Activity** ━━━━━━━━━━━━━━━

The context of social work 1

The role of a social worker is governed by professional standards, a code of ethics and it is subject to legal duties. Legal duties are the requirements set out in an act of law which provides social workers with a mandate to undertake assessments, conduct inquiries into safeguarding concerns and, sometimes, take more punitive action (such as removing a child from their family, or using the law to hospitalise someone who is mentally unwell). Using law, social workers are agents of the state (Howe, 2008).

Now read the paragraph again and consider if it is descriptive or analytical. It is descriptive! Now read the paragraph in Box 4.8.

― 🖎 ― **Box 4.8 Activity** ━━━━━━━━━━━━━━━

The context of social work 2

The role of a social worker is governed by professional standards, a code of ethics and it is subject to legal duties. Legal duties are the requirements set out in an act of law which provides social workers with a mandate to undertake assessments, conduct inquiries into safeguarding concerns and, sometimes, take more punitive action (such as removing a child from their family, or using the law to hospitalise someone who is mentally unwell). As such, social workers have been described as agents of the state, fulfilling a 'controlling' role to ensure that communities comply with society's cultural norms and values. As such, social workers play a pivotal role in maintaining societal harmony.

The paragraph in Box 4.8 incorporates analysis. However, the paragraph offers one particular view. Alternative, contrasting perspectives add another layer of depth (see Box 4.9).

━ 🖊 ━ Box 4.9 Activity ━━━━━━━━━━━━━━━━━━━

The context of social work 3

The role of a social worker is governed by professional standards, a code of ethics and it is subject to legal duties. Legal duties are the requirements set out in an act of law which provides social workers with a mandate to undertake assessments, conduct inquiries into safeguarding concerns and, sometimes, take more punitive action (such as removing a child from their family, or using law to hospitalise someone who is mentally unwell). As such, social workers have been described as agents of the state, fulfilling a 'controlling' role to ensure that communities comply with society's cultural norms and values. It has been claimed that social workers play a pivotal role in maintaining societal harmony (Smith, 2016). However, in a UK-wide study on social workers' norms and attitudes to the role and function of the profession, the majority of participants (87%) indicated that social workers do not see themselves as agents of social control, but as agents of social change, supporting and empowering families and adults to address their problems and improve their quality of life (Jones, 2018).

The third example offers different perspectives and is supported by evidence from research. This illustrates the way in which different authors can be used to add greater depth and detail in the critical analysis. This is explored in more detail next.

Synthesis

A good essay will consider different perspectives, theories or arguments, but with a clear indication of your position. A strong argument will contain critical and evaluative elements with alternative points of view. By adding different perspectives, you are presenting a balanced view and demonstrating that you can engage with and interpret different ideas, rather than merely arguing from a one-dimensional position. Similarly, in practice, those social workers who can look at a problem from different viewpoints will produce better, more holistic and informed assessments and interventions. They will be able to justify their decision-making while being open and accountable.

Use different authors to contrast and contradict the points being made; this creates a critical debate. For example:

> 'Smith (2013) observes that self-neglect in an older person is a matter of choice and lifestyle, whereas Rogers (2017) argues that self-neglect can be indicative of risks to health and well-being and needs further investigation'.

Along with 'whereas', use 'on the contrary ...', 'although ...', 'conversely ...', 'nevertheless ...', 'in contrast ...', 'instead ...', 'offering a counter-perspective ...', 'others argue ...', 'alternatively ...'. Effectively, what you are doing is synthesising a range of knowledge about the issue/problem. As you move towards the end of your essay, you should be able to clearly articulate what each perspective has to offer, and if there are gaps in knowledge or existing theories, say so.

Danger point: making unsubstantiated claims

We have referred to the issue of making unsubstantiated claims throughout this chapter so far, but because it is such a common problem in students' academic writing, we wanted to emphasise the need to avoid this by adopting good habits from the start of your studies. Unsubstantiated claims come in different forms, but generally they can be both broad, sweeping statements and very specific and detailed points that have no substance; that is, within the body of writing there is no evidence or support for such claims. You will need to use different forms of knowledge to provide support your arguments (see Chapter 2 for a discussion about forms of knowledge). For instance, formal knowledge, such as theory, can help to support your analysis and any claims that you make. This gives validity and authority to your discussion.

Take the following example of an unsubstantiated claim: 'Grief is a hard process and never ends'. We might use theory to support such a claim as follows:

> 'Kübler-Ross's model offers a way of understanding how people move through five stages of grief before they reach acceptance and, as such, this supports the view that people who experience loss can demonstrate resilience to overcome their grief.'

Citations, referencing and avoiding plagiarism

As noted earlier in this chapter, whenever you present an idea/theory/model from someone else's work, then you need to acknowledge this. This is called a citation and typically contains a surname, publication date and, where you have included a direct quote, a page number (all contained within brackets). All references are then listed at the end of your essay as the 'reference list'. This is not a bibliography; it is something different. A bibliography is a list of materials that you have used as background reading, but that you have not necessarily cited in your essay. You do not usually need to include a bibliography in your written work (unless you are directed to in the assignment guidance). Including citations and producing a reference list accurately and consistently is another academic convention that you should aim to get right from the start of your studies. Most universities adopt a particular style, the Harvard system, but there is a divergence in the formats that universities use. Therefore, particular attention should be paid to specific university referencing guidance.

Referencing serves a function as it provides an acknowledgement for the authors who have produced the work that has informed your work. It signposts the reader to the original source of the ideas or arguments being presented and enables them to find that work if they wish. It may be that the reader is not sure that your interpretation of the literature is correct, and they wish to return to the original to check your understanding, and providing the reference enables a quick and easy way to find the work. In terms of plagiarism (copying someone else's work), using referencing properly, in part, helps to show where you have found the material in your essay. If you are using direct lines from a source, then ensure that you put these in quotation marks and reference the page that you found them. This is important as it avoids questions about the authenticity and originality of your own writing.

A common question that is asked pertains to the number of citations/references that are expected. There is no clear answer as it depends on the assignment task, and the field or discipline. A lack of citations often results in weaker writing. Sources, such as journal articles, help to add criticality, contemporary perspectives and empirical evidence and you should attempt to use these routinely.

SUMMARY

The art of critical writing is something that can be developed with practice, particularly if you pay attention to academic conventions and issues of synthesis and structure. Being successful at academic writing involves a range of skills, including: cognitions (being able to understand the assignment task); planning and organising material; the application of English language (vocabulary, grammar, syntax, use of punctuation, etc.); the selection and appraisal of evidence; the ability to develop an argument; and structuring a line of reasoning towards a conclusion. In other words, there is a lot to manage in producing academic writing, and the sooner that you embed good practice, the easier it will be, and the more successful you will be in developing a strong writing style. You should maintain a sense of audience (that is, who you are writing for) and of the task (frequently return to the assignment title and any guiding material).

Having read this chapter, you should be able to:

- Understand the importance of planning and organisation for academic writing
- Understand the difference between description and analysis
- Develop the confidence to write critically
- Embed critical thinking in academic writing
- Recognise the importance of valid substantiation when constructing arguments
- Appreciate the importance of academic conventions.

FURTHER READING

Bottomley, J., Cartney, P. and Pryimachuk, S. (2018). *Academic Writing and Referencing for Your Social Work Degree*. St Albans: Critical Publishing.

Cottrell, S. (2017). *Critical Thinking Skills* (3rd edn). London: Macmillan International.

Gillett, A., Hammond, A. and Martala, M. (2009). *Successful Academic Writing*. Harlow: Pearson Education.

PART III

CRITICAL THINKING AND ANALYSIS IN PRACTICE

5

CRITICAL REFLECTION

THEORETICAL BACKGROUND

- Experiential learning
- The socio-political contexts of practice
- Power and oppression
- The use of self
- Participation and equality

RELEVANCE TO SOCIAL WORK THINKING AND PRACTICE

- Demonstrating core social work competencies
- Evaluating the way that social work practices affect you and the experiences and outcomes for people you are training to support
- Considering whether your practice is specific and supported by evidence from experience, as well as being grounded in theory and research
- Verifying the effectiveness of your practice with the support of experts by experience

REAL-WORLD CHALLENGES

- Limited skills in reflection
- Limited knowledge of social work theory and research
- Time constraints
- Low value placed on the process of critical reflection
- Seeing reflection as private
- Not using models of reflection to develop specific, measurable, achievable, realistic or timely learning objectives

Introduction

This chapter will help you to understand why critical reflection is so central to the professional values and ethics that underpin social work education and practice. Essentially, practising critical reflection, while studying social work at university and on placement, serves to facilitate opportunities for you to embed the ability to evaluate into the praxis of your professional identity. As you become an autonomous, independent critical thinker, you should be developing the knowledge, values and skills needed to reflect on, think about, and confidently articulate the perspective and socio-political context of the individuals, families and communities you are training to support. You should also be aware of the complex and often competing roles of social work, and the lasting impact of your own social work practice on others.

Developing the knowledge, values and skills needed to reflect on, think about and confidently articulate matters related to social work practice can be difficult. The ability to reflect well does not always come naturally. It is a process that must be learnt and developed. This is one reason why you are encouraged to keep reflective logs while on placement and approach some social work assignments through a lens of sustained reflection.

To facilitate opportunities for you to become a critically reflective practitioner, this chapter will introduce you to some of the theories and methods that underpin critical reflection. Focusing on the primary assumptions of critical reflection 'in' and 'on' practice, this chapter will provide you with the practical tools needed to enable you to engage in ongoing reflection and critical inquiry concerning social work practice in both action and process. By the end of the chapter, you should have developed the confidence to begin to consider how your own personal beliefs and values, assumptions, and social conditioning impact on you and the people you are training to support. As you should be concerned with democratising social work too, this chapter will also provide a framework which you can go on to develop as you progress through your studies. First, it is important to engage in an exercise of self-reflection and consider what type of reflector you might be (see Box 5.1).

 Box 5.1 Activity

What style of reflection do you prefer?

Before you consider the process of critical reflection in much more detail, it is helpful to consider what type of reflector you are. Review each of the statements adapted from White et al. (2006) to identify your preferred style of reflection.
Do you:

- interpret social work situations by using your intuition and feelings?
- work in a way that feels natural to you and often struggle to support or substantiate your practice with evidence from experience, theory or research?

- value the principles of equality and ensure that you work with all people in the same way, never treating people differently?

If you have answered 'yes' to all of these questions, you might be an 'intuitive' reflector. Do you:

- measure your success as a social worker by your ability to pass assignments?
- work in a way that is supported with evidence from experience, but not theory or research?
- value the principles of equality and try to work in different ways with different people to accommodate differences?

If you have answered 'yes' to all of these questions, you might be a 'surface' reflector. Do you:

- constantly think about how social work practices are affecting you and the experiences of and outcomes for people you are training to support?
- believe that your goal as a social worker is to continually improve practices and outcomes for individuals, families and communities?
- ensure that your practice is specific and supported by evidence from experience, as well as being grounded in theory and research?

If you have answered 'yes' to all of these questions, you might be a 'social work' reflector. Do you:

- always engage in ongoing reflection and critical inquiry concerning your own practice?
- continuously examine and seek to verify social work ideologies and practices with the support of experts by experience?
- consciously consider how your personal beliefs and values, assumptions, family imprinting and cultural conditioning impact on your approach to practice?
- concern yourself with promoting democratic ideals of social work theories and methods in all aspects of your life?

If you have answered 'yes' to all of these questions, you might be a 'critical' reflector.

The styles of reflection presented in Box 5.1 suggest four primary approaches to social work thinking and doing. Evidence to support the categories and compartmentalisation of intuitive reflection, surface reflection, social work reflection and critical reflection has been collected from several sources. Some sources of information about reflection in social work have been taken from serious case reviews or public inquiries (see Munro, 2011), and other sources of information about the ways in which professionals reflect have been taken from research (see Jansen, 2018).

If we consider the various sources of information used to create the four styles of reflection listed in Box 5.1, we must recognise that some preferred styles of reflection may not be adequate for professional social work practice. As a minimum standard, and certainly by the time you become an early career social worker, you should be able to state with developing confidence that you are a 'social work' reflector.

As a 'social work' reflector, you should be constantly thinking about how law, policies, theories and methods are affecting the experiences and lives of the people you are training to support. You should recognise that good social work practice is not determined by module marks or a degree classification, but by your ability to form effective relationships with others. You should also prioritise the need to continually improve your own approaches to practice and seek new and innovative opportunities for social change. You should be able to describe stated social work values to others and to articulate why your beliefs and positions about practice are specific and supported by evidence from experience, as well as being grounded in theory and research. As a 'social work reflector' who values the opportunities enabled through reflection, you should be able to view practice as a multi-dimensional event by connecting the use of self to, and within, the ethics, duties of care and lived experience of those people who you are training to support.

At this point in your social work education and training, the style of 'social work' reflection should be the gold standard – in other words, the level of reflection that you should be aiming for. Once you become a proficient and capable 'social work' reflector, you will be well on your way to becoming a 'critical' reflector. Our guess, however, is that you are reading this chapter because you are probably an 'intuitive' or 'surface' reflector – and that is perfectly natural too.

Starting out on your social work career, you will be most likely to interpret social work situations (at first at least) without achieving thoughtful connections to other events or circumstances. Your response to social work education and practice might be reactive, believing that opportunities for social change are beyond your control. As you are learning to do social work, your beliefs and positions about social work practices might be generalised too and not supported by evidence from experience, theory or research. You might be beginning to realise that equality requires you to work with different people in different ways, but you might not feel confident to transfer and apply your developing knowledge values and skills into practice.

If the skills associated with 'intuitive' reflection or 'surface' reflection do resonate with you (and, again, be honest), because your decisions are determined by how you feel about a situation, or because you can do social work but you cannot describe how you do it, or because the skills associated with 'social work' reflection appear too distant, there is no need to panic or worry. Remember, you are on a learning journey – a journey that is defined by learning. Again, reflection is a skill that needs to be developed. It also requires practice.

Recognising that you might struggle to apply theory to practice, that socio-political contexts of practice may not always be clear to you, a feeling of anxiety about doing social work is perfectly acceptable at this stage of your career. It is acceptable because you recognise these challenges as real, and in reading this chapter, you are seeking ways to become a more effective reflector. The situation might be different if you prefer 'intuitive' reflection or 'surface' reflection because it is easier, and for this reason, you are not prepared to admit this fact or do anything about it. Honesty is the first step to becoming a critical reflector (and *ipso facto* a safe and effective practitioner). You must be able to recognise, validate and then speak about potential limitations in the ways that you think about yourself and others and the way that you do social work. If you know that you can struggle to think about how social work practices are affecting the experiences of and outcomes of others, if you know that you struggle to recognise the values that guide social work practice, if you know that you struggle to substantiate your beliefs and positions about practice with evidence from experience, if you struggle to ground your arguments in theory and research, and, in knowing these things you struggle to accept, discuss or plan to improve your own work, you might be failing in your most basic duty as a student social worker.

Accepting that the style of 'social work' reflection should be the gold standard, then, requires us to journey to that destination. In this chapter, our journey begins with some contextual knowledge of what critical reflection is, and why it is done. We will then scope out a brief theoretical definition of reflection, those theories used to inform practice, and then consider the methods of reflection to facilitate opportunities for you to build, and then speak about some of the knowledge, values and skills needed to be a proficient, capable and complete 'social work' reflector.

Theoretical context

Critical reflection in social work draws upon critical social theory (Brown, 2017) (the analytical frameworks, or paradigms, that are used to study and interpret social phenomena), informed by postmodernism (Giddens, 1990) and post-structuralism (Bourdieu, 1977), to make links between personal and structural power (see Box 5.2). Taken together, these theories are used in reflection to enable personal and collective capacities for social change. In social work, critical reflection incorporates these theories into a very practical understanding of how to deconstruct, interrogate and reconstruct professional practice. These models of reflection also aim to facilitate opportunities for social workers to ensure that the people who they are working to support experience their own critical intentions, their own hopes, their dreams and their aspirations, rather than the recommendations of the professional (Allen and Riding, 2018). Used effectively, critical reflection can enable practice wisdom through an ever-increasing awareness of empowerment and new innovative, creative and anti-oppressive ways of working and being (Rogers et al., 2016).

━━ 🔄 ━━ Box 5.2   Theory explained ━━━━━━━━━━━━━━━━

Postmodernism is an approach to social work thinking and practice that enables you to explore and understand the various ways in which social–political and economic trends

(Continued)

(Continued)

might affect the people you are training to support and, therefore, the task, purpose and function of social work. Postmodernism provides a framework for you to think about how theory and practice interact and how evidence-based approaches to practice evolve as you develop knowledge from experts by experience. Centralising the expert by experience is crucial in postmodern social work activity, and ultimately its relative success. Postmodernism also provides you with some ideas about how to work with people in practice.

Questions:

- What social work theories and methods do you think align with postmodernism?
- What do you need to do to learn more about postmodernism?

Post-structuralism is an approach to social work thinking and practice that enables you to explore and understand the importance of individual lived experiences within individual contexts. Post-structuralism in social work assumes the need to trust but verify knowledge by speaking to those people you are training to support, to deconstruct modalities of power by emphasising the need for active participatory approaches. Post-structuralism is driven by individual strengths and motivated by the solutions provided by the expert by experience.

Questions:

- What social work theories and methods do you think align with post-structuralism?
- What do you need to do to learn more about post-structuralism?

The critical nature of social work practice posits that social workers, with a commitment to personal development, enablement and wellbeing, who value a commitment to social justice and social change, need to understand the difference between critical reflections 'before' action, 'during' action and 'after' action (Allen, 2018). This is because the purpose of critical reflection is not only to improve practice (although that is certainly part of it), but also to change and challenge dominant power relations and power structures, and to create possibilities to practise more critically in whatever context social work operates, and at each discrete stage ('before' action, 'during' action and 'after' action). Critically reflecting on social work practice 'before', 'during' and 'after' an example of work done involves, and is heavily reliant on, the recognised and valued need to change or develop practice and to reduce any power inequalities that might determine coercive or oppressive decisions.

We will not develop much in the way of reflection before action in this chapter. Recognising that critical reflection is a skill that needs to be developed, we believe that the skills needed to reflect 'on' action and 'in' action are most accessible. We will wait until Chapter 8 to discuss reflection 'before' action.

Reflection on action

While social work practice operates at three distinct stages – 'before' action, 'during' action and 'after' action – most social work students are examined on their ability to reflect on the situations that they have encountered after an event. This approach is often referred to as **'reflection on action'**. It is particularly encouraged by the theoretical models advanced by Gibbs (1988) and Kolb (1984), for instance. In such cases, reflection on action involves reflecting on how practice can be developed or changed after the event. It requires you to reflect on what you have done in order to (re)discover how your actions may have contributed to the outcome.

Reflection on action is arguably the easiest form of reflection. Often, 'intuitive' reflectors and 'surface' reflectors prefer this approach as social work theories, methods, law, policies and even codes of practice can be applied retrospectively. Being able to 'reflect on action', as presented in the activity in Box 5.3, is a minimum requirement of social work education.

 **Box 5.3 Activity**

Reflection on action

Try to recall an example of practice and interaction with another person, or a memorable learning experience, and then complete the model of reflection adapted from Gibbs (1988) in Figure 5.1.

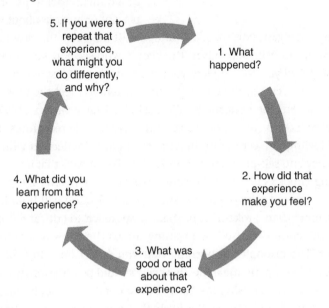

Figure 5.1 Reflection on action

Danger point

When it comes to reflection, complacency could make you arrogant. You might believe that if you were to encounter a similar situation in the future you might not do anything differently (because you are fantastic) and that you have nothing further to learn. Arrogance, or overconfidence, can also contaminate case notes and case files as any blame for a lack of progress, cooperation or passive acquiescence is placed squarely with the people you are working to support. In this situation you might be tempted to say things like 'This person cannot be helped because they do not want to help themselves' or 'Mr X is aggressive and has challenging behaviour'. Conversely, anxiety could make you worry that your practice is not good enough. You might use Gibbs (1988) to validate your low confidence as your feelings about being an 'impostor' restrict your ability to identify your own strengths. In both examples, of arrogance or low self-confidence, emotional intelligence – the capacity to be aware of, control and express one's emotions, and to handle interpersonal relationships judiciously and empathetically – is an essential characteristic of social work and the ability to critically reflect (Allen, 2018).

Kolb and Fry's (1975) four-stage model of learning and Schön's (1983) conceptual development of reflection in action and reflection on action are often regarded as a foundation for experiential learning. Indeed, the overlap between Gibbs's (1988) model above and Kolb and Fry's (1975) model is not surprising, given the main function of reflection: to learn from one's experiences, seeks to provide a basis that can deepen an understanding of actions and events.

As a minimum requirement, reflection on action is a skill that each social worker should be able to demonstrate. Reflection on action and the model presented above often form the basis of reflective logs in practice, for example. While Gibbs's (1988) or Kolb and Fry's (1975) reflective cycle above can be useful in making you think through all the phases of an experience or activity, it can be a difficult tool to use if you are complacent or anxious about your practice.

In addition to arrogance or low self-confidence, it might be the case that your tutor, practice educator, or onsite supervisor (the people who support you during your work placement) has asked you to complete your reflective logs at the end of the day. But it is also likely that the end of the day is the time when you feel the most tired or most eager to go home. For the critical education scholar Henry Giroux (1997), the timing of experiential reflection (reflection on action) is crucial. He recognises that your own thoughts and feelings are central to the process of critical reflection which is 'the stuff of culture, agency and self-production' (1997: 110). This means that if you seek to reflect on action using Gibbs's (1988) or Kolb and Fry's (1975) reflective cycle when you are tired, stressed, worn out, distracted or rushed, your reflection will hold little meaning, enabling little more than a tokenistic or shallow approach to critical reflection.

Reflection on action can also lose meaning unless the focus of attention is specific and significant. The examples of learning that you reflect on using Gibbs's (1988) or Kolb and Fry's (1975) experiential reflective cycle should be noteworthy – those practice or learning experiences that will most likely be memorable to you. If you start to reflect on every small example of learning, it is likely that the process of reflection will lose relevance and interest. If you are unsure about what you ought to be reflecting on, perhaps speak to your tutor, practice educator or supervisor.

Finally, reflection on action can lose meaning if the focus of attention remains solely drawn to your own individual practice. As you may remember from the above discussion, 'social work' reflection requires you to draw upon the lived experience of those people who you are working to support. It also requires you to consider theory, research, as well as the feedback provided to you by others. While Gibbs's (1988) or Kolb and Fry's (1975) model of reflection can enable you to consider your role in experiential learning, they do not easily enable you to include other, equally important perspectives. For this reason, reflection on action should be complemented by incorporating as many different perspectives as possible. One model that you could use to include and draw upon the lived experience of those people you are working to support, together with social work theory, research and the feedback provided to you by others, has been provided by Brookfield (1995). Although primarily developed for teacher training, it is easy to adapt this model for social work.

Brookfield's four lenses

The goal of the 'social work' reflector using Brookfield's (1995) model is to garner an increased awareness of thinking about and doing social work from as many different vantage points as possible. To this end, Brookfield proposes four lenses that can be engaged by social workers in a process of critical reflection. Starting with autobiographical reflection – like that suggested by Gibbs (1988) or Kolb (1984) – it also includes the views of the people you are working to support, the views of your mentor or colleagues and the view of the theoretical literature. Cogitating upon these processes provides the foundation for good social work and the means to become a 'social work reflector'. Have a go at completing Brookfield's (1995) four-lens model as detailed in Box 5.4.

Undoubtedly, reflection on action using Brookfield's (1995) four-lens model is harder than using Gibbs's (1988) or Kolb and Fry's (1975) model because it requires you to engage in the processes of self-reflection. It requires you to include the feedback from the person you have worked with and peer assessment. It also requires you to engage with scholarly literature. But by using this model to reflect on action, you might be able to hold up your philosophical ideologies and practices for more meaningful examination and verification than you might achieve with any other model.

Reflection on action is the retrospective contemplation on practice to uncover the knowledge that was or was not used in a particular situation (Allen, 2018). By analysing and interpreting the information recalled, you should be able to use Gibbs's (1988), Kolb and Fry's (1975) or Brookfield's (1995) experiential reflective cycle to effectively move away from 'intuitive' reflection or 'surface' reflection. This is because you should also develop an awareness of how a situation might have been handled differently if you had applied a different set of knowledge, values and skills. While the ability to reflect on action is arguably one of the minimum requirements of social work education and practice, representing a skill that each social worker should be able to demonstrate, it requires care and consideration. To consider what these considerations might be, we have prepared a reflection-on-action danger points list.

— Box 5.4   Activity ■■■■■■■■■■■■■■■■■■■■■■■■

Brookfield's (1995) four-lens model

Try to recall an example of practice, and interaction with another person or a memorable learning experience, then try to complete the model of reflection adapted from Brookfield's (1995) in Figure 5.2.

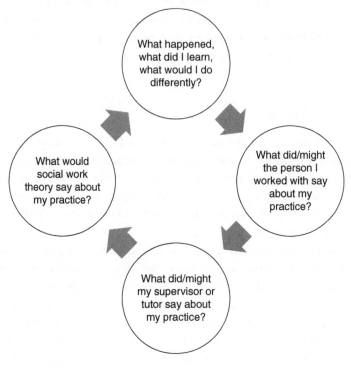

Figure 5.2   Four-lens model

Source: adapted from Brookfield (1995)

Reflection in action

The second and more difficult stage of critical reflection is '**reflection *in* action**'. It involves two distinct components. First, it requires you to think about what you are doing when you are doing it. Second, it requires you to think about how you are doing social work, including a constant evaluation of the practical knowledge, values and skills that underpin your practice. It requires you to link what you know with what you do as you construct your practice as an active agent who can substantiate the application of law, policy, theory and methods based on the uniqueness of the person who you are working to support (Schön, 1983), rather than some broadly related esoteric theory.

Reflection in action arguably requires you to possess an advanced ability to link the epistemological origins of social work (see Chapter 3) with its subsequent application so that the theories and methods used to underpin all aspects of your own practice are suitable and appropriate to any moment. Reflection in action also requires **reflexivity**. To be reflexive, you should be able to recognise your own and other people's frames of reference, to identify any dominant discourses and carefully examine the way you seek to make sense of the lives of others. You should also seek to recognise how your own bias, discriminatory perspectives, stereotypes and pre-judgements can contaminate the

Danger point

- Do not attempt to think about or write reflective logs or accounts if you are tired
- Do not blame others for any situation or limitation in your own practice
- Do not rush your reflection
- Do not reflect on minor learning experiences
- Do not supress feelings of anxiety or distress
- Do not keep your reflections private – share them in supervision
- Do not minimise the feedback of others
- Do not forget to plan future learning goals
- Do not forget to include knowledge from theory and research and feedback from others

Try not to be too hard on yourself!

social work (more about this in Chapters 6 and 8). Most importantly, reflection in action requires you to disrupt assumed causal relations so that you make a conscious effort to reflect on the various ways in which power relations operate to impact on your work, and the way that you are being perceived, in real time.

Utilising the four steps listed in Box 5.5, try to recall a time where you were required to reflect in action and carefully consider the way that you made decisions during an example of direct work.

 Box 5.5   Activity

Reflection in action

Step 1: Try to recall an instance where you were engaged in direct work with another person (on placement or in simulation at university).

Step 2: Think about how you planned this direct work. If you feel that this direct work went well for you, try to write down the things that you did that made the situation effective. If you are not happy with the experience, note what you might have done differently to improve the outcome.

Step 3: Consider which social work theories and methods you set out to use. Did you use these theories and methods, or did you have to change your tactics? If you did not change your tactics, how did you know the theories and methods that you were using

(Continued)

(Continued)

were effective? If you did change tactics, explain the process or experience that led to your making this decision.

Step 4: Write a list of the various ways in which reflection in action helped you to manage this example (or not) of direct work.

Reflection in action is an essential skill that enables you to measure and evaluate social work practice in real time. It is very difficult, however, to achieve reflection in action if your knowledge of social work theories and methods is limited. The ability to reflect in action means that knowledge of how to think about and do social work has first to be known before it can be made critical. In other words, the laws, policies, theories, methods and codes of practice must first hold meaning and then be meaningful to you before you can become a critical reflector. It stands to reason, for example, that a person might not be able to critically reflect on the pragmatic application of psychodynamic interview techniques in an assessment if they do not know what psychodynamic interview techniques are, and for that matter, have never experienced psychodynamic interview techniques for themselves. For this reason, it can be hard to reflect in action if you are not confident to practise social work in the first place.

As reflection in action is hard, chiefly because it requires knowledge about the law, policy, theory and methods, you might be tempted to prioritise the opportunity to reflect *on* action, as per the minimum requirement. However, if that is a decision that you take, you will almost certainly continue to operate within the bounds of 'intuitive reflection' or 'surface reflection', satisfied with the ability to only articulate knowledge, values and skills after the event. If this is the case, any reticence to reflect in action will present a fundamental problem for safe, effective and professional social work practice in the future.

The primary importance of reflection in action is that social work is a sense-making activity. It requires you to make constant use of your senses to understand the situations that you encounter to arrive at safe and effective assessments (more on this in Chapter 6). When visiting people who experience poverty, violence, substance dependency, crime, or systematic social marginalisation, for example, there may be times when you feel out of place, a 'stranger' or outsider. Confronted with the experience of culture shock, you can perceive the situations through a discriminatory lens (Allen, 2018). As you might feel 'out of place' while visiting people in their home, your non-reflected personal values and value judgements become a measure of risk that is often used to justify the need for formal social work involvement, or not. Rather than working to understand the challenges that were being faced by individuals, families and communities, you could (albeit unwittingly, we are sure) represent a further layer of structural discrimination because your initial impressions or judgements reflect your own internalised feelings, rather than the lived reality of the people or situations that you are working to assess.

Danger point

- Do not practise social work without prior planning
- Do not undervalue the skills needed to think quickly to evaluate whether or not your plans are working
- Do not blame others if your intervention goes wrong
- Do not assume that your lived experience alone will make for good social work practice
- Do not ignore the expert by experience and their ability to shape and determine the direction of your practice
- Do not forget to record examples of reflection in practice in your reflective log and do not forget to share these in supervision.

Try to be reflexive in your approach to social work, and remember that what works for one person might not work for another.

Using critical reflection to plan future learning

The strengths facilitated by opportunities to reflect in and on practice can be sustained and developed if a meaningful approach to action planning is achieved. By importing the theoretical principles of task-centred practice (Rogers et al., 2016) to your own professional development, you can use the information and opportunities for learning uncovered through the process of critical reflection to map out future learning objectives. If you then share these action plans with your tutor, practice educator or supervisor, you may begin to demonstrate your ability to reflect and plan. As your reflective logs are personal but not private, you may also begin to see the value of critical reflection as you begin to structure discussions during supervision about your actions, your experiences and learning, and your future learning goals. Why not use the template provided in Box 5.6 to set out and develop specific, measurable, achievable, realistic or timely learning objectives? If you can, base these objectives on the discoveries that you made during the reflection-in-action and reflection-on-action activities.

 **Box 5.6   Activity**

Using reflection to identify a learning plan

Use Table 5.1 to plan out your own learning goals. By way of example, we have provided two illustrations of potential tasks to help you get going.

(Continued)

(Continued)

Table 5.1 Planning your learning goals

Who	What	When	Where	Why
e.g. Me	e.g. Revise theories and methods related to motivational interviewing	e.g. Before the next home visit	e.g. Borrow a book from the library	e.g. To develop my confidence to work in a person-centred way
e.g. Practice Educator	e.g. Provide feedback on my practice following direct observation	e.g. Next supervision	e.g. Supervision	e.g. To validate my own reflections

SUMMARY

Learning how to become a critically reflective practitioner requires you to be prepared and able to listen to yourself as well as to those whom you are working to support and those who are supporting your learning journey. If you are seeking opportunities to achieve the level of 'social work reflection', you might do well to deconstruct knowledge, to read research, social work theories and methods, and to speak with honest confidence about your own practice.

Having read this chapter, you should be able to:

- Recognise the limitations of 'intuitive reflection' and 'surface reflection'
- Understand that critical reflection requires honest emotional intelligence
- Develop an awareness of the models used in critical reflection in and on practice
- Embed critical reflection into your own social work practice
- Recognise the importance of seeking or imagining feedback from others
- Recognise how stereotypes and presuppositions could contaminate your practice.

FURTHER READING

Brookfield, S. (1995). *Becoming a Critically Reflective Teacher*. San Francisco: Jossey-Bass.

Gibbs, G. (1988). *Learning by Doing: A Guide to Teaching and Learning Methods*. London: Further Education Unit.

White, S., Fook, J. and Gardner, F. (2006). *Critical Reflection in Health and Social Care*. Maidenhead: Open University Press.

6

PROFESSIONAL JUDGEMENT AND DECISION-MAKING

THEORETICAL BACKGROUND

- Risk and power
- Trusting intuition but verifying knowledge
- Confirmation bias
- Cognitive behavioural theory
- Procedural, questioning and exchange models of assessment

RELEVANCE TO SOCIAL WORK THINKING AND PRACTICE

- Transparency in professional judgement
- Verified knowledge
- The theorised link between thoughts, feelings and behaviour
- Relationship-based practice

REAL-WORLD CHALLENGES

- Low confidence assisted with a developing knowledge of social work theories and methods
- Busy caseloads
- Reluctance to speak honestly about thoughts, feelings and behaviour

Introduction

Eileen Munro (2011) has pointed out that the most common and problematic tendencies in social work reflection are the limited confidence to review judgements and plans once a view has been formed on what is going on. This limitation occurs when individuals struggle to notice or dismiss evidence that challenges an initial impression. Where an initial perception is contaminated by prejudice, there is a heightened risk that judgements will be made about a situation regardless of any evidence or counter-evidence that may be available.

This chapter will provide a view of the techniques and strategies that can be used to ensure that decisions are being made upon verifiable fact, rather than unsubstantiated supposition. Problematising the notion of a 'gut reaction', this chapter will encourage the application of specific methods that could be applied to critically reflect on and analyse evidence while defending against the pressing challenge of **confirmation bias**.

Decision-making and risk

Social work is becoming increasingly focused on the need to predict, manage and reduce risk. The knowledge, values and skills needed to assess the likelihood of harm, and then the ability to plan and manage services or organised approaches to work that seek to keep people safe, are essential social work characteristics (Rogers et al., 2016). Yet, the decision-making processes that social workers use to assess and respond to risk are as complex as they are contentious.

Social work is proud of its theories and methods for practice. Often developed and adapted from theoretical approaches that have been established in disciplines related to health, psychology and sociology, these theories and methods provide an evidence base from which to gather information and then justify action. The fact that there are so many different theories and methods that a social worker can use to gather information and then justify action, however, creates serious concerns for consistency.

The question we need to ask, therefore, is whether social work should be a natural activity. Is it good enough to apply the same communications skills that are applied in everyday life in the assessment of risk, or are additional skills required? Of course, this is a rhetorical question. As you will have

Danger point: low confidence in applying social work theories and methods

Not only will the experience of social work change for the people you are training to support as they encounter different social workers, namely because every social worker is different, but the application of the theories and methods used to underpin practice will be different according to individual experience and expertise of the practitioner. Early-career social workers often tell us that the task of thinking about applying a theory and method to inform and guide practice can become problematic as they feel that their engagement is becoming formulaic. In other words, they say that to apply a theoretical framework to a conversation or thinking process is not natural.

probably guessed from reading the preceding chapters, social work is proud of its academic history and the critical need to learn about and develop the knowledge, values and skills needed to do social work. While some people who are not social workers might be good at listening, demonstrating empathy, care and compassion, they might struggle to also see and assess risk against mitigating social, psychological and biological factors. They may be good communicators, but they may struggle to facilitate opportunities for change through close collaboration and co-production. They might be able to decide, but they may be unable to justify and defend this decision under cross-examination.

The knowledge, values and skills that make social work a distinct and protected profession, however, are not applied without contention. The fact that social workers work differently and apply so many different theories and methods without consistency means that decisions must always be critically considered. Let us consider why critical reflection is important in decision-making with the following example.

 Box 6.1   Case study

Unprepared and ill-equipped

A student on their final-year placement is developing their knowledge, values and skills at a local fostering agency. They have a very busy diary and have been asked, at very short notice, to assess a woman living in the local area who has registered her interest in becoming a short-break carer for children with life-limiting physical, sensory and multiple impairments. As well as being very busy with lots and lots of other assessments and university work, this is the first time that the student will have completed an assessment of a potential carer on their own.

The student arranges an appointment to conduct the assessment with the woman on the phone. During the conversation, the student struggles to hear what the woman is saying because a dog is barking very loudly in the background.

On the day of the assessment, the student arrives at the address by car. The woman lives in a high-rise block of flats that looks like it needs modernisation. The student becomes stressed as they struggle to find a car parking space. When the student eventually manages to park the car, a group of young people approach and ask the student if they have a spare cigarette. The student says that they do not smoke. The student thinks that the young people are very rude and intimidating.

The student walks to the block of flats, stepping over rubbish strewn around the area. The student notices that the grass verges are overgrown. They also observe dog mess all along the pavement. The student begins to feel nauseated.

At the high-rise flat, the student struggles to see the numbers on the intercom as it has been vandalised. After a few minutes, the student presses the buzzer for the flat where the prospective carer is thought to live. There is a brief exchange over the intercom, but again the social worker struggles to hear what the woman is saying as

(Continued)

(Continued)

the dog is barking so loudly. After a brief pause, the front door of the flats clicks open. The student begins to feel scared.

Inside the entrance hall, standing in front of the lifts, the student reads offensive words graffitied on the wall. The entrance hall smells of urine. The student also notices that the lifts are broken, meaning that they must climb the stairs up to the eighth floor. The student remembers how heavy their bag is as the young people who were outside by the car come rushing in shouting and swearing, nearly knocking the student over. The student wants to run home.

Hot and out of breath, the student finds the flat where the woman lives. There is racist graffiti on the front door. Reluctantly, the student knocks on the door.

Straight away a dog starts to bark and jump up at the back of the door. The student hears the woman shouting at the dog, 'Get down, you daft animal!'

The woman opens the front door and the dog escapes, jumping up at the student and almost knocking them off their feet. The dog, a German shepherd, which when on its hind legs is the same height as the student, licks and smells and barks. Too embarrassed to do anything and unable to get the dog down, the student freezes. The student is now petrified.

The woman grabs the dog by the collar and shouts, 'Get down, you daft animal!' The woman then invites the student into her home. By this time the student is very distressed. They have already decided that this woman is not suitable to be a short-break carer for children with life-limiting physical, sensory and multiple impairments.

In the flat, the dog sits on the sofa next to the student. It is breathing heavily. Wanting to take flight, the student rushes the assessment. The student knows that they have a lot of other (more important) work to do and thinks that this visit is a waste of time. After six minutes of polite conversation, the student says goodbye to the woman (and the dog) and rushes back to their car. Back in the office, the student tells the practice educator that the woman in the flat would be an unsuitable short-break carer.

Questions:

1. Why do you think the student decided so early on that the woman was unsuitable?
2. Do you agree that the student made good use of their professional judgement?
3. How might the prospective carer describe her experience of the assessment?

In many different situations, the professional judgement and decisions that a social worker makes are central to the way that services and outcomes are shaped and delivered. However, as social work is a 'sense-making activity' that is practised differently by different people, there is huge room for inconsistency and prejudice.

The fact that social work practice is so variable also means that the people you are working to support will have different experiences of receiving social work. If we consider the example in Box 6.1, we might consider that the student was so quick to judge because of the socio-economic profile of the area, and, of course, because of the large dog. Perhaps the student was not familiar with socio-economic disadvantage. Perhaps they had no 'proximity' or prior lived experience of being in a high-rise block of flats. Perhaps they did not like or were afraid of dogs. Whatever the reason, throughout the visit there was a clear association between the student's thoughts (I am busy, I am in a strange environment, I do not like dogs) and how they felt (intimidated and scared) and behaved (unprofessionally and dismissively). Just as cognitive behavioural theory (Gambrill, 2007) might predict, the thoughts and feelings of the student directly determined their behaviour. The point to make in this regard is that if the same assessment had been conducted by another student, who themselves lived in a high rise with a large dog, the professional judgement and decision-making process might have been quite different. The subjective nature of social work, and the fact that a professional judgement can be based on or influenced by negative or positive thoughts, gut feelings, intuition, personal tastes, or individual opinion, is one of the reasons why social work can be seen by some of those people you are working to support as being unfair.

 Box 6.2   Key point

Social work as a sense-making activity

When we describe social work as a sense-making activity, what do you think we mean? Well, social work requires us to gather verifiable evidence from the people we are working to support. We gather information through our five senses: the things we see, the things we hear, the things we touch, smell and even taste.

See. During an assessment, we often consider the environment within which the person being assessed lives. We look at their home. We also look at the person. We look to assess their physical appearance. We look at the interactions the person has with us and with those around them. Being able to see the situation of the person we are working to support is a skill because what we see forms part of our assessment.

Hear (listen). Social work requires us to hear because it requires us to listen. Often during social work assessments, we will ask people to describe what life is like for them. We try to understand what life might be like through their eyes. Being able to listen to what the person we are working to support is saying is a skill because what we hear forms part of our assessment.

Smell, touch and taste. While assessing some situations, smell, touch and taste can be crucial to our ability to make sense of what may be going on. Some things that we smell, and some things that we touch, can highlight and demonstrate living conditions and environments. The things that we taste (sometimes the metallic taste of our own adrenalin) can also be a way to gather information.

(Continued)

(Continued)

Questions:

1. If we gather information using our senses, how do we interpret those things that we see, hear, smell, touch and taste?
2. Is there room for a sixth sense (gut feeling) in social work?

One way to reduce the subjective nature of social work is to ensure that decisions are made within the bounds of law and relevant codes of behaviour, conduct and ethics. **Human rights** and equality legislation and duty serve to provide a legal framework from within which social work should operate. If the woman in the above example was assessed as being unsuitable because of her ethnicity, sexuality, age, disability, gender, religion or any other defining characteristic, the student would be breaking the law. The fact that law exists, however, does not mean that people are free from discrimination in social work. Law underpins safe and effective practice, but it does not mean that all social workers do not discriminate.

Social work regulation and associated codes of professional conduct also apply to guide a minimum expectation of what social work should and should not be. A commitment to social justice, advocacy, fair representation and an informed professional judgement, that can be substituted and verified by evidence, are examples of practice governance that seeks to create consistency. While the 'doing' of social work might be as different and as unique as the individual social worker and therefore vary from one person to another, the scope of work is required to operate within the boundaries of ethical and virtuous practice. Indeed, there is no room for decisions that are unethical, or which demonstrate a lack of virtue, in social work.

In addition to law, social policy and social work governance, one further way to reduce the subjective nature of social work is to apply evidence-based approaches to decision-making processes. However, the evidence base is only as good as the social worker who applies it. We will now explain the reason why.

Grounding professional judgement in evidence

When we mention 'professional judgement' and 'decision-making', we are talking about assessment. 'Assessment', a word that is synonymous with 'evaluation', 'judgement', 'appraisal' and 'opinion', demonstrates a fundamental aspect of social work. Every day, a social worker will be making a professional judgement about risk, eligibility for services, resilience, capacity and change. In many situations, experienced social workers will have the power to make a decision that will have a lifelong impact on another individual. If we recall the above example of the woman wanting to become a carer for children living with a life-limiting impairment, we can see how the student exercised the power to deny this opportunity. Whether this decision was right or wrong is not being presented here for consideration because the point that we are trying to make is related to the use of power.

We will consider the position of radical and deviant social work later, but for the time being we will simply observe that the presence of power, the power to make a professional judgement, and to be paid for exercising this power, can corrupt. While the student above might recommend the refusal of an application of a prospective carer because they have a large dog (and the student is afraid of dogs), they might approve another carer because they remind them of a close relative (and they love that relative very dearly). The student might not admit to the fact that their decision has been influenced by a feeling (fear versus love) because if they did they would be working outside of the bounds of law and social work governance.

> ## Danger point: using your thoughts and feelings to substantiate decisions
>
> Let us be clear that feelings do influence decision-making processes in social work in the same way as they influence decision-making processes in our personal lives. This is natural. The difference between the personal and professional spheres is that the best social workers can talk about their feelings with their supervisors so that decision-making processes (and assessments) can be held open for critical review. If the student in the above example told the practice educator that they decided that the woman would be an unsuitable carer because of perceived socio-economic disadvantage, and the fact that they did not like dogs, you might rightly imagine the outcome of the placement to be quite different. Critical reflection recognises that feelings may be personal, but in social work these feelings should not be private and never kept secret.

Again, social work must operate within the bounds of law and good governance. For this reason, social workers should be mindful that the decisions that they make are lawful, ethical and virtuous. It is often the case, however, that many of the people whom social workers work to support complain about the service that they receive. In many cases, these complaints pertain to the decision-making process itself (Allen, 2018).

According to Howe (2008), professional judgement and decision-making in social work rely on the ability to collect, collate and analyse information. Taking note of the Russian proverb, *doveryai no proveryai*, social workers also should 'trust but verify'. They trust first impressions and the information that they initially receive, encounter or uncover, but they also verify whether the information is true. The skills needed to trust but verify can be demonstrated in the ability to use verifiable information to form a professional judgement and in the commitment to seek out new evidence that could be used to either disprove, inform, or change the initial judgement. Going back to the flat on the eighth floor of the high-rise flat, the student who decided that the woman would be an unsuitable carer should have sought out evidence to disprove the initial impression, rather than confirming the same through feelings that were associated with the 'environment' (and the dog) within which the woman lived.

If we were to attempt to identify a single problematic aspect of social work reasoning, the risk of confirmation bias would be one of the main candidates for consideration.

Many social work academics and practitioners have written about this bias (see Gray et al., 2017), and it appears to be sufficiently influential in the social work decision-making process that many assessment frameworks have been designed to counteract its effects. Confirmation bias has been used in the social work literature to refer to a variety of phenomena. Here we take the term to represent the occasion, like that shown in the example above, when social workers look for and only include evidence that confirms their initial impressions.

Reducing confirmation bias in social work is essential to ensure that professional judgements and decisions demonstrate a true reflection of individuals' lived experience. As social work is a sense-making activity, however, confidence in the ability to defend against the risk of confirmation bias is difficult to state fully. One way to achieve a confirmation-bias-free assessment is to remove the human element. If the assessment process is free from human intervention, it is free from prejudice. But can a social worker make a professional judgement or decision without physical intervention? The simple answer is 'yes'.

Artificial intelligence and social work

One solution to the challenge faced by the student in the above example is to remove the sense-making activity. If the student had not had negative thoughts, felt under pressure, busy, hot and bothered, scared and intimidated, the outcome of that meeting and the subsequent decision might have been very different. If, rather than relying on the student's professional judgement, a robot were programmed with an algorithm to identify the suitability of a short-break carer, the opportunity for confirmation bias would be removed.

If the image of a robot conducting an assessment in social work seems like science fiction, it is important to note that predictive algorithms are already being promoted by some social work departments as they seek to determine who is and who is not eligible for scarce social care services. Webb (2006) reasons, for example, that in the context of reduced spending in public services, predictive computerised algorithms can be a method of assessment that ensures that services are provided based on verified information rather than on perceived need. As perception is variable, artificial intelligence ensures that decisions are objective and free from confirmation bias. Let us consider artificial intelligence in the social work decision-making process with the following fictional example.

 Box 6.3 Case study

An assessment using artificial intelligence

A woman uses her computer and accesses a social work department web page to register her interest in becoming a short-break carer for children with life-limiting physical, sensory and multiple impairments. The web page directs the woman to another electronic application form.

The form asks the woman to fill in her address. The algorithm then uses this information to assess the suitability of the area based on socio-economic data, including local crime rates. The algorithm also cross-references the address with local and national police databases to check for criminal records of the woman and her relatives. It accesses the woman's medical files to check her medical history and completes a credit score to evaluate her financial situation. Using the address, the algorithm searches the electoral register, driving licence database and Home Office to identify any evidence to suggest why this woman should not be considered as a potential carer. If the algorithm finds information about a criminal record, poor health, potential relationships with others involved in crime, and so on, her application will end.

The form asks the woman a series of questions related to relationships that she has with others. The algorithm uses her responses to scale her attachment to her parents and provides a score on what type of attachment she has. Unless the woman scores 100%, indicating that she has a 'secure' attachment, her application will end.

The form then asks the woman to provide information about any pets she has. The algorithm uses that information to risk-assess suitability based upon the dog breed and type. If the woman says that she has a dog, in this case a German shepherd, the algorithm considers the size, known aggression, information about whether the dog moults and so on, to decide whether it would be safe for the dog to be around a child with life-limiting physical, sensory and multiple impairments. If the risk was too high, the woman's application will end.

Finally, the form asks the woman to write a summary of why she wants to be considered for a position as a short-break carer for children with life-limiting physical, sensory and multiple impairments. The algorithm then analyses her response to arrive at a score out of 100. If the woman scores less than 80, her application will end.

Questions:

1. What are the strengths and limitations of this fictional example?
2. What might be the ethical concerns regarding the use of artificial intelligence in this way?
3. How might the prospective carer describe her experience of the assessment?

The above fictional example of artificial intelligence in social work is not wholly imagined. Artificial intelligence is making significant developments in the prediction of suicide, mental health, propensity to crime, reoffending and more (Abbas et al., 2016). Studies have been conducted with people living with dementia who utilise artificial intelligence and robots to assist in their activities of daily living (Jiang and Yang, 2017). What is more, the self-assessment model is used even more frequently in all areas of social work (Tambe and Rice, 2018). Rather than relying on social workers to go out on home visits, the individuals you are training to support are asked to complete their own assessment and either post it to the office or email it in for consideration. Fortunately, artificial intelligence has not been applied to all social work decision-making and information is still collected through human engagement. The risk of confirmation bias therefore continues.

The solution to reducing confirmation bias is seen by some policy-makers, social work academics and practitioners as the adoption and application of a standardised assessment framework. Ideally, if 100 social workers were to assess the same individual, not only should the individual experience consistency, but also the outcome of the assessment should be the same. This solution is known as the 'procedural model of assessment' (Smale and Tuson, 1993).

Procedural models of assessment

The procedural model of assessment can support decision-making that is perceived as reasonable and reasoned. According to Smale and Tuson (1993), it is essential that the social work profession uses a procedural model of assessment to undertake work competently and for it to have credibility. Used well, a good procedural assessment supports the comprehensive gathering of information and helps to order and analyse the information that is gathered (Rogers et al., 2016). What is more, it relies on a series of closed questions, where the answer can be limited to specific responses. It stills requires a social worker to use their human agency to gather and analyse information, but because the procedural assessment follows a structured approach the opportunity for confirmation bias is reduced. Let us consider procedural assessments with the following example.

 Box 6.4   Case study

A procedural assessment

A student on their final-year placement is developing their knowledge, values and skills at a local fostering agency. They have a very busy diary and have been asked, at very short notice, to assess a woman living in the local area who has registered her interest in becoming a short-break carer for children with life-limiting physical, sensory and multiple impairments. As well as being very busy with lots and lots of other assessments and university work, this is the first time that the student will have completed an assessment of a potential carer on their own.

The student arranges an appointment to conduct the assessment with the woman on the phone. During the conversation, the student struggles to hear what the woman is saying because a dog is barking very loudly in the background.

The student plans the visit very carefully. There is no information about the woman on the social work office file, so the student invites a colleague to attend the visit so that they can go in a pair. The student uses an internet street map tool to view the local area at street level. The student notices that parking might be an issue, so decides to go on the visit using public transport.

As the student is being supported by a colleague, they feel less intimidated by the area. They do not feel threatened by the young people and laugh when they see the lift is out of order. They then get to the eighth floor (feeling healthier for it!) and notice that there is racist graffiti on the front door. Reassured by the presence of the colleague, the student knocks on the door.

Straight away the dog starts to bark and jump up at the back of the door. The student hears the woman shouting at the dog, 'Get down you daft animal!'.

The woman opens the front door and the dog escapes, jumping up the student and almost knocking them off their feet. The dog, a German shepherd, which when on its hind legs is the same height as the student, licks and smells and barks. The student's colleague fusses over the dog. It gets down and goes back inside the flat.

In the flat, the dog sits on the sofa next to the student. It is breathing heavily. The student, confident with the colleague's support, asks what the dog's name is. The woman says that the dog is called Jess and that she is a rescue dog. Having suffered terrible abuse in its early life, the woman says that the dog suffers from anxiety but is very loving and protective. She says that the dog is particularly good with her grandchildren. The woman says that since having the dog, she has not been bothered by the hooligans who wrote racist remarks on her front door. The woman also explains that the flats are in a poor state of repair and that she is looking forward to moving to a new home in the next few months under a new, local government initiative.

The dog goes to sleep, and the student begins to relax even more. The student starts the assessment using a procedural model that has been developed by the placement. The student writes down the responses to the following questions as the woman speaks:

1. What is your full name, address and date of birth?
2. Do you have any medical conditions?
3. Who else lives here in the flat with you?
4. What is your religion?
5. Do you speak any other languages?
6. Do you have any children?
7. How many bedrooms do you have?
8. Does the flat have any existing aids and adaptations?
9. Would you be willing to have aids and adaptations fitted if required?
10. Are you married, in a civil partnership or similar relationship?
11. Can you provide the names and addresses of two persons who will provide personal references for you?

At the end of the assessment, the student reads out the responses to verify accuracy.
   Questions:

1. What are the strengths and limitations of this example?
2. How might the prospective carer describe her experience of the assessment?

Danger point: limitations with procedural models of assessment

The main limitation of procedural assessment methods is that they can become prescriptive and formulaic. For this reason, some of the people you are training to support can find the assessment process clinical and insensitive. If a person wants to talk about matters that are not required as a part of the procedural assessment methods, some social workers might tell the person they are working to support that the conversation is 'going off track'.

By taking a structured approach to the process of gathering information (as shown in the above example), it could be argued that assessment becomes more objective, less subjective, and as a result replicable. A hundred social workers could visit the woman, ask the same 11 questions, and arguably get identical responses. The structured approach also helps to identify the relevant information that is needed to make an informed decision. A broader understanding of person-centred theory and communication theory (see Gray et al., 2017) might help in the application of a procedural assessment model, but it certainly does not underpin it. As the approach to assessment provides a standardised approach to gathering evidence, the social worker's gut feelings and initial impressions can be trusted but then verified by what is seen, heard, smelt, touched and even tasted. Confirmation bias can be reduced as the structured approach to gathering information means that relevant information is provided, and irrelevant information is discounted. From the perspective of the people you are training to support, Allen (2018) shows that this assessment process seems fairer and less intrusive as the individual can be told the questions being asked are the same questions that are asked to everyone else.

Procedural assessment methods also require minimal skill. Apart from the ability to ask a question, record a response, and then verify the accuracy of the recording at the end of an assessment (a crucial phase that is often missed out), no specialist knowledge of social work theories and methods that extend much further than Egan's (2002) SOLER model are required (see Box 6.5).

 Box 6.5 Key point

Egan's (2002) SOLER model

Gerard Egan has published a model that uses the acronym SOLER. It is not without limitations, but he (and some social work theories) recommends using it when conducting an assessment:

- S – **S**it side on to the person you are assessing
- O – Sit with an **o**pen posture; no crossed legs or folded arms, for instance
- L – **L**ean forward in your chair slightly
- E – Maintain a comfortable degree of **e**ye contact
- R – **R**elax

While there is an opportunity in procedural models of assessment, those that rely on a series of closed questions where the answer can be limited to specific responses and where confirmation bias is reduced, the responses cannot provide a full or rich description and understanding of an event. If we consider the procedural assessment model that was used by the student in Box 6.4, it would not be consistent with this model to ask the woman why she wants to become a short-break carer for children with life-limiting physical, sensory and multiple impairments. This is because the response that the woman provides cannot be limited to a specific response. What is more, if 100 social workers were to ask the woman what her motivation might be for becoming a short-break carer for children with life-limiting physical, sensory and multiple impairments, the answers will almost certainly vary.

In the same way that social work is a sense-making activity, where we seek to make sense of another's situation through the things that we see, hear, touch, taste and smell, the people you are working to support will be making sense of you too. We frequently tell our students that the people you are working to support will often remember you for the rest of their lives because you will make an impact on them. Some people do not welcome social workers, and the decisions that they must make. Others do. The point is just that as social workers work differently, so different social workers will be perceived differently (more on this in Chapter 8). While a procedural assessment model, like that shown above, might help the social worker to gather rudimentary information, it cannot capture phenomena like motivation or the ability to nurture and love a child in an equal way. What is needed instead is an alternative approach to professional judgements and decision-making. It is here that radical social work and deviant social work come centre-stage.

Procedural, questioning and exchange models of assessment

According to Carey and Foster (2011), radical social work and deviant social work are two sides of the same coin. They are labelled as such because they require a social worker to depart from procedural models of assessment. Where an assessment without any framework can lead to prejudicial judgements, a structured procedural approach can identify consistent, but limited responses. A semi-structured approach, however, as seen in procedural, questioning and exchange models of assessment, centralises the knowledge and expertise (and indigenous knowledge) of the person being assessed to identify mutually agreed outcomes and decisions (Davies and Gray, 2017). As assessment is not something that should be done *to* people, it is a process that should be done *with* people (Rogers et al., 2016). For this reason, the need to combine elements of questioning and exchange models with procedural assessments is vital.

Not only can the risk of confirmation bias be reduced because the person taking part in the assessment is viewed as the 'expert by experience', but also enabling the person to tell their story in a way that suits them, and not the system, demonstrates respect and minimises condescension. What is more, the combined use of procedural, questioning and exchange models of assessment means that people are viewed as active

 **Box 6.6 Theory explained**

Table 6.1 highlights the differences between the procedural, questioning and exchange models of assessment.

Table 6.1 Procedural, questioning and exchange models of assessment

Assessment type	Who is the expert?	The role of the social worker
Procedural model	The agency and the individual who is asking the questions and recording the answers	The social worker is required to ask the questions and record responses in a structured and systematic way
Questioning model	The social worker	The social worker uses their skills to uncover information that might not be immediately obvious
Exchange model	The person being interviewed	The social worker facilitates the opportunity for the person being interviewed to tell their story in their own terms so that any solutions or goals can be set and owned by the individual

agents whose lives are impacted by and responsive to broader examples of structural discrimination (Rogers et al., 2016). If we review the example of the student's visit in Box 6.1 through a procedural, questioning and exchange modelled lens, it is possible to argue, for example, that the student themselves reinforced a layer of structural discrimination. By applying procedural, questioning and exchange models of assessment, the student could demonstrate an early glimmer of radical social work by acting to reduce the impact of their own confirmation bias. They might trust their gut feelings based upon what they see, hear, touch, taste and smell, but they then verify the same with the questions that they ask. In many cases, these questions will not be listed on a pre-prepared assessment form.

Box 6.7 Case study

A combined approach to assessment

Once in the flat, the dog goes to sleep, and the student begins to relax even more. The student starts the assessment using a procedural model that has been developed by the placement. The student writes the responses down to the following questions as the woman speaks:

1. What is your full name, address and date of birth?
2. Do you have any medical conditions?

3. Who else lives here in the flat with you?
4. What is your religion?
5. Do you speak any other languages?
6. Do you have any children?
7. How many bedrooms do you have?
8. Does the flat have any existing aids and adaptations?
9. Would you be willing to have aids and adaptations fitted if required?
10. Are you married, in a civil partnership or similar relationship?
11. Can you provide the names and addresses of two persons who will provide personal references for you?

Once the above information has been recorded, the student puts the assessment form away. The student takes a deep breath and says, 'So, tell me why you are motivated to become a short-break carer.'

Other questioning and exchange modelled questions that the student asks include:

1. You have provided the names of two references. If I were to speak to them on the phone and ask them whether you would be a suitable short-break carer, what do you think that they would say?
2. Why do you think you would be an excellent short-break carer?
3. What aspects of being a short-break carer do you think you would find hard?

At the end of the assessment, the student asks the woman if she has any questions or would like to provide any further information.

Questions:

1. What are the strengths and limitations of this example?
2. How might the prospective carer describe her experience of the assessment?

Taking such an approach to assessment means that the theories and methods used to conduct an assessment must be confidently known and confidently applied. In the example in Box 6.7, the student uses some aspects of motivational interviewing techniques to apply questions based on narrative theory (see Rogers et al., 2016). Not everybody will feel comfortable asking these types of questions and not everyone will feel comfortable answering these types of questions. But, as we can see from the example, a detailed understanding of the situation is vital if a reliable professional judgement and decision can be made. These detailed responses can only really be generated through a procedural, questioning and exchange model of assessment.

By engaging in an exchange model of assessment (as shown in the question 'What aspects of being a short-break carer do you think you would find hard?'), the student in Box 6.7 is more likely to understand the situation of the person whom they are working to support as if seeing the world through their eyes. This technique enables some of the people whom social workers are working to support to talk about things that they have kept secret or never shared with anyone before. For this reason, social workers occupy a privileged position. But by engaging in and hearing people's lived experiences and life stories, the opportunity for confirmation bias creeps back in. As the woman in the example tells her story, the student and the woman might begin to feel that they are developing a relationship with one another. The student might laugh with the woman, might cry with the woman, might even begin to feel emotionally connected to the woman. Here a decision of suitability might be made because the woman reminds the student of a close relative (of whom they are fond). If the student is not careful, they might trust their initial instinct to recommend the approval of the carer without fully verifying the information presented. While procedural, questioning and exchange models of assessment might work to the betterment of a process, they might also work to the detriment of professional judgement and decision-making, particularly if the person's responses are not fully explored or confirmed. The woman in our example might say that she has no current medical conditions that could jeopardise her parenting capacity, but medical records might show that she is living with epilepsy. As a single short-break carer, this information might be vital and could only really be verified through medical records or a health-care professional's assessment. Equally, the woman might say that she would be an excellent short-break carer because she is a trained nurse. If this information were trusted but not verified, the impact of this trust on the children that she might look after in the future could be significant if she was not telling the whole truth. It is for these related reasons that an exchange model of assessment can become deviant unless a healthy scepticism is used to verify responses (Allen and Riding, 2018).

For Carey and Foster (2011), deviant social work is often defined as small-scale acts of resistance, subterfuge, deception or even sabotage that are typically hidden yet scattered throughout parts of the social work labour process. The example of the student's visit to the prospective carer in Box 6.1 is a clear illustration of this principle. Instead of conducting the assessment properly, the student failed in their basic duty to practise within legal and good governance frameworks. The student had decided that the woman would not be suitable even before she had met her. However, according to Allen (2018), deviant social work also emerges from the shadows when those feelings that accompany human engagement turn from positive to negative responses. Throughout your career, you will work to support people

Danger point: the danger of emotive action

Whether your thoughts and feelings towards the people you are working to support are positive or negative, you must take steps to ensure, as hard as it can be, to remove emotion from your decisions. You must work with people, apply your senses, develop relationships that are critical to procedural, questioning and exchange models of assessment, but you must try hard not to be emotive. You should trust your gut feeling, your intuition, your initial impressions, but you must always verify whether these perceptions are true.

whose behaviour you find confusing and offensive. Some of the people you work to support will tell you that they do not like you. Some will even threaten you or try to hurt you. What you must not do is allow your feelings to contaminate your professional judgement and decision-making. If you did, your professional judgement could be compromised, as suggested in the body of work on deviant social work (Carey and Foster, 2011).

SUMMARY

Social work is a relationship-based activity, and you will be required to work with others to gather information and formulate decisions for action. As you develop your relationships with others, it is likely that you will also develop feelings about the people you work with, and the situations they are in. It is OK to become emotionally involved in social work. Social work is, after all, a vocation. However, there is a line of professional capability that must not be crossed.

As you develop your knowledge, values and skills and your ability to review judgements and plans once a view has been formed on what is going on, supervision will provide you with a valuable opportunity to substantiate the decisions that you are making. While it is natural to develop feelings about the people you work with, and the situations they are in, you must not (as the student did in the example in Box 6.1) allow confirmation bias to characterise your work. The important proviso in all social work activity is that you ensure that you can discuss the associated links between your thoughts, feelings and behaviour, as assumed in cognitive behavioural theory (Gambrill, 2007), openly and honestly, and without fear of criticism. It is only acceptable to develop feelings about the people you work with, and the situations they are in, if you talk about them in supervision. It is not OK to keep your thoughts, feelings and actions secret. In relation to radical and deviant social work (both examples we have shown here), the need for transparency is essential. Our thoughts can influence not only the way we feel, but also the way we behave. Sometimes this behaviour will be to the betterment of social work practice, but sometimes to the detriment of practice too.

Having read this chapter, you should be able to:

- Recognise the power associated with professional judgement
- Consider the strengths and weaknesses associated with procedural, questioning and exchange models of assessment
- Critically consider the relationship between thoughts, feelings and behaviour
- Identify the opportunities associated with radical social work and the dangers associated with deviant social work.

FURTHER READING

Allen, D. (2018). Roma people: Are discriminatory attitudes natural? In K. Bhatti-Sinclair and C. Smethurst (eds), *Diversity, Difference and Dilemmas: Analysing Concepts and Developing Skills* (pp. 77–94). London: Open University Press.

Deacon, L. and Macdonald, S. (2017). *Social Work Theory and Practice: Mastering Social Work Practice*. London: Learning Matters.

7

CRITICAL ANALYSIS: WORKING WITH RISKS AND STRENGTHS

THEORETICAL BACKGROUND

- Critical thinking
- Ecological systems theory
- Strengths-based perspective
- Risk

RELEVANCE TO SOCIAL WORK THINKING AND PRACTICE

- Approaches and models for practice
- Analysis, evaluation and synthesis
- Applying forms of knowledge
- Embedding analysis in assessments
- Working with risks and strengths

REAL-WORLD CHALLENGES

- Limitations in ability to apply theory and knowledge to real-world situations
- Demands of the job mean that knowledge is applied uncritically
- Becoming overly concerned with risk assessment and its control

Introduction

This chapter builds on the ideas presented in all chapters so far in terms of critical thinking, professional judgement and decision-making to consider skills in critical analysis, but here we locate the chapter's focus in the context of working with both risks and strengths. In doing so, we highlight some of the debates centring on the assumption that the complex mix of individual practice, organisational demands and socio-economic structures might not always support good and effective practice. In these debates, it is easy to develop a sense of defeat as these focus on limitations rather than strengths. But in this chapter, we suggest that this is not necessarily the case. We believe that being a social work practitioner gives you the opportunity to promote change by working collaboratively and in partnership with the people you are training to support.

In positioning analytical skills as a tool to identify and develop professional practice and in the pursuit of good outcomes for the people you are training to support, in this chapter we will provide you with lots of case study examples to highlight how critical analysis is easily embedded in good, ethical practice. Social work is a profession that struggles to celebrate success, but this chapter will encourage you to consider adopting a more positive approach to risk through strengths-based thinking so that you can see yourself, your learning and your role in promoting social justice and change in a more constructive and balanced way.

What is critical analysis?

Various sources of knowledge (research and public inquiries, for example) have drawn attention to the centrality of critical analysis, but these have also highlighted how social workers can struggle to integrate analysis into their written records and reports. For example, Sidebotham et al.'s (2016) meta-review of serious case reviews (SCRs), which are conducted when a child dies or is significantly harmed and there is learning to be had, found that within published SCRs there were frequent acknowledgements of how the move from description to analysis was inconsistent in social worker reports. However, while Sidebotham et al. noted that 'there were examples of over-long unfocused reports', they also recognised that 'there were also good examples of reports which offered a clear analytical overview' (Sidebotham et al., 2016: 218). Thus, Sidebotham et al.'s overview suggested that there are inconsistencies and a lack of a consensus about what constitutes critical analysis.

So, let us start with a clear understanding of what is meant by critical analysis. 'Analysis' refers to the study or examination of something in order to gain a better understanding, explanation or description. Taking a further step, the notion of 'critical analysis' includes a questioning element in that you do not take something at face value but try to think about and weigh up different elements or perspectives on something. In this sense, it is not 'critical' in the negative sense, but in an academic sense. As such, an analysis that is critical is significantly helped along with the input of theory and empirical knowledge as this steers you towards critical analysis using evidence and taking different perspectives. See Box 7.1 for an example.

 Box 7.1 Case study

Deena Hall

On Monday morning Deena tells you that she has a black eye from walking into a door. You know there is a history of domestic abuse and the World Cup final was televised on Saturday, and you suspect Deena's partner, Joe Jones, was binge drinking while watching the match in the pub as this is what he frequently does.

You have a good working partnership with Deena and would like to think that you can have an open dialogue. You know that there are implications for the family in terms of whether or not a domestic abuse incident has occurred as there are two children who live in the Hall/Jones family: 5-year-old Logan and 12-year-old Chantal. The family currently receives social work support at a lower level (on a *child in need* basis) because of the history of domestic abuse and substance misuse. If there were more concerns, this might be elevated (to a *child protection* basis). Deena's adult child, Jasmine, lives in a nearby village with her father and step-family.

Stop and reflect:

Do you believe Deena's version of events?

If you answered 'no' to the question above, then you have probably knowingly or instinctively used particular forms of knowledge to assist your analysis and judgement, including practitioner knowledge (knowledge of the Hall/Jones family and their history) and research knowledge (the link between sports events and spikes in domestic abuse incidents, and the many impacts on children who live with domestic abuse). We will return to the Hall/Jones family later in this chapter.

From describing and summarising to analysing situations

Providing a full description and summary of a situation is very different from providing an analysis. This point is linked to decision-making as in both scenarios (summarising and analysing) decisions can be made; the difference is that where an analysis has been done, a more informed decision will be made using professional judgement and evidence (see Chapter 6). While the types of questions answered when providing a summary involve 'what is happening and who is involved?', an analysis asks 'why is this happening?', 'what is the impact?', 'how is this significant?' and so on. See Box 7.2 for a practice example illuminating the differences between summarising and analysis.

 Box 7.2 Case studies

From summarising to analysis

Summarising a case and making recommendations: Logan Jones

Logan is a 5-year-old boy living with his father, Joe Jones, his father's partner, Deena Hall, and her 12-year-old daughter, Chantal. Logan is in the reception class at his local school. Staff have noticed a decline in his presentation; sometimes he is smelly and seems to be wearing the same clothes as the day before. Sometimes he is bubbly, boisterous and demanding of attention, but at times he is withdrawn and quiet. The Hall/Jones family live in a two-bedroom flat on a local estate, and Logan shares a bedroom with Chantal. There are not many toys in the flat, and it is sparsely decorated. Joe has been out of work for some time, struggling to find employment as a plasterer. Deena used to work as the receptionist for the local swimming baths, but it closed and she has not worked since. Deena has experienced depression on and off for years and does not seem to be coping well at the moment. Both Deena and Joe have been known to misuse alcohol. I recommend a case review.

Analysing a case and making recommendations: Logan Jones

Logan is a 5-year-old boy living with his father, Joe Jones, his father's partner, Deena Hall, and her 12-year-old daughter, Chantal. Logan is in the reception class at his local school. The family has a history of domestic abuse, but both Deena and Joe claim that there have been no incidents since April when Joe began the perpetrator programme offered by an anti-abuse charity. Deena recently presented with an injury which she explained as resulting from an accident. However, staff at Logan's school have noticed a decline in his presentation (he is frequently grubby and smelly) and erratic behaviour (sometimes boisterous and sometimes withdrawn). Research suggests that for children living with domestic abuse there are often emotional, social and behavioural impacts (CAADA, 2014).

In addition, both Deena and Joe have not been in employment for several months, adding to the family's stress and lack of resources. Deena's mental health was better in May when Joe had begun to attend the perpetrator programme, but I have noticed a distinct decline in the past month, and Deena admitted that her depression is worse and this is affecting everyday coping. In addition to Deena's admission that her mental health suffers when Joe is being abusive, there is a large research base to illustrate the significant mental health impacts of living with domestic abuse (Howard et al., 2013). Overall, this suggests that domestic abuse is still occurring in the family home, with clear impacts on Deena and Logan. I recommend a case review.

Analysing risk

The concept of risk is part and parcel of everyday activity for social workers. What constitutes a risk and how we respond to it (through assessments, decision-making, interventions and planning) can vary, and this is influenced by a whole range of contextual detail including the complex mix of individual practice, organisation boundaries and socio-economic structures. Moreover, risk is dynamic, rather than static, and so the assessments and decisions that we make one day may need to change in response to the presenting situation the next day. In general, risk is considered to be a situation or phenomenon that can result in danger or harm. Of importance is the recognition that it is easy to consider risk as having negative implications, whereas in actuality there are positive risks to be taken in life (see Box 7.3 for a case study example). A negative approach is easy to adopt in social work as the very nature of our tasks means that we are dealing with problems and it is important to remain alert to the capacity for pathologising and attributing blame. This is not what social work is about. In actuality, it can be common for social work assessments to identify levels of risk that are acceptable or even no risk at all. What is important, however, is that as practitioners we remain alert to the many influences that impact on our ability to assess risk and make decisions based on reasonable judgements and verifiable evidence. In this section we would like you to consider risk and **positive risk-taking**, which is the notion that measuring risk involves balancing the positive benefits gained from taking risks against the negative effects of attempting to avoid risk in its entirety.

 Box 7.3   Case study

Jasmine and positive risk-taking

Twenty-two-year-old Jasmine lives with her family (father, step-mother and three younger step-siblings) in a village on the outskirts of a big market town. Jasmine has learning disabilities. She has recently finished a college course which she loved, attending it with a group of friends that she had made when at the local school for children with additional needs. Jasmine's dream is to get a job and earn some money for herself. Jasmine decided that she wanted to volunteer in a charity shop in the nearby town to get work experience as she knew another person with learning disabilities who had managed this. However, Jasmine's family were very concerned about her ability to manage the responsibility of this (the travel, lunches, managing money, etc.). Jasmine wanted to prove that she could make this change to a more independent way of life.

Jasmine's family eventually agreed, and Jasmine began voluntary work on three days a week. She found the first few weeks to be very challenging. Travelling alone on the bus was the most difficult part, although Jasmine had travelled alone before after she had undertaken travel training. Jasmine found all aspects of public travel to be

(Continued)

(Continued)

stressful (getting to the bus stop on time, boarding alone, managing money and looking after her return ticket). She became very tired and low. Jasmine wanted to quit, but her family had been convinced that voluntary work was a good idea and negotiated a new arrangement with Jasmine: she would do one day's voluntary work a week and would have help with transport (her father would drop her off and she would get the bus home). This worked well and gradually Jasmine built up her confidence to travel alone again. This boosted her resilience, and she maintained this one day a week at the charity shop. After two months Jasmine began to take the bus for both journeys.

Questions:

1. Was a positive risk-taking approach appropriate for Jasmine? Why or why not?
2. Can you identify the negative and positive risks to Jasmine (think of positive risks as opportunities) when she began voluntary work? How did these change over time? Which risks changed over time, and were they negated altogether, or was this a change of level of risk?

These questions are designed to help you critically analyse the case study. They are the types of questions that you might ask yourself in social work practice.

Analysing risk can be a complex process as risk can be difficult to measure, unpredictable and unstable. Risk analysis can therefore present a number of challenges but, in terms of risk assessment, professional judgement and decision-making, there are some theoretical models that can be helpful and will steer you to take a critical, analytical approach. These theories can serve as prompts for your assessment of situations in a specific way and by asking particular questions. We will introduce you to a popular social work theory, **ecological systems theory** (EST), which requires an analysis of the different elements at play in everyday contexts; see Box 7.4 for a definition and explanation of this model and how you can use it to enhance your analysis of a situation.

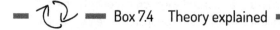 **Box 7.4 Theory explained**

Ecological systems theory

Ecological approaches enhance an understanding of people and the ways in which they interact with their environment. Such approaches adopt the idea that society is a network of different structures, or systems, which interact on different levels. Bronfenbrenner (1979) developed this idea in his conception of ecological systems theory (EST). His aim was to enhance our understanding of child development and the factors that affect this. EST has been very influential in social work and other disciplines which utilise theories of human development. Bronfenbrenner's EST can be understood in terms of how separate elements (family, school, community) are positioned in systems (micro, meso, exo, macro) and how these interact. Figure 7.1 shows these systems as a layer of concentric circles; each system has influence over the life of the individual at the centre of the diagram. Each system can be summarised as follows:

- Microsystem: people or structures in a person's immediate life.
- Mesosystem: an individual's interactions with their community and surroundings.
- Exosystem: secondary systems that impact on an individual's life – for example, family social networks, the wider neighbourhood, parent's workplace or unemployment.
- Macrosystem: structural systems that impact on an individual's life – for instance, societal norms and values, gender, ethnicity, or the legal system.

There is another level, the chronosystem, which considers the influence of time or relationships or incidents that are in the past, but which may continue to affect the individual.

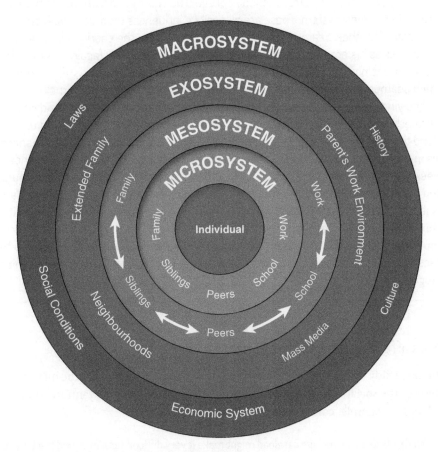

Figure 7.1   Bronfenbrenner's ecological systems theory

(Continued)

(Continued)

The value of applying this theoretical model in social work, and in an analysis of an individual's situation, is that it can help a more critical analysis by prompting the practitioner to consider influences in an individual's life that are not immediately evident. It prompts you to identify risks in each system (or the interactions that occur within or across systems), but also to identify protective factors (relationships or structures that can mediate identified risks).

 Box 7.5 Case study

Applying theory

Suppose that Jasmine is at the centre of Figure 7.1. In Jasmine's microsystem are her family and her friends from school/college. The charity shop where she works is located in her mesosystem. These are all positive influences (or protective factors).

Jasmine's father, Seamus, begins to drive Jasmine to the charity shop. Seamus can do this as his employer allows him to go in late on that day (again, positive elements in Jasmine's exosystem). Jasmine's social worker, Simeon, is disheartened when Seamus tells him that he can no longer commit to this weekly journey.

Applying ecological systems theory helps you to explore what is a risk and what is a protective factor. It may prompt you to ask further questions of Seamus to understand this further. When Simeon contacted Seamus to explore why he had changed his mind, Seamus admitted that his employer had decided that his late arrival once a week was now inconvenient, particularly as other employees had asked for 'favours' and this had become difficult to manage. This example demonstrates how secondary systems located in the exosystem (that is, ones that do not immediately or implicitly impact on an individual) can have considerable influence. In this way, EST directs you away from a narrow analysis, thinking about the individual only, to orient you to consider individuals as part of multi-faceted systems with complex interrelationships (Rogers et al., 2016).

Factors affecting the quality of analysis

In the case study of Jasmine, there are various factors that could affect the quality of the analysis of the social worker, Simeon (not just the options for intervention, as noted in Box 7.3). For example, consider these different influences:

- *High caseload.* Simeon's high caseload might make it very difficult for him to find the time to speak at length with Seamus to find out the real reason for this change, and this would impede his analysis of the situation.

- *Agency influences.* As noted above, there might not be any agency finances to help with taxis, or the policy might not support this intervention.
- *Media.* Simeon is new to working with the team, having just transferred from an older persons' social work team. How might media representations of people with learning disabilities affect Simeon's analysis in relation to Jasmine and risk?
- *Beliefs and norms.* Simeon has a cousin with autism, and the whole family are very protective of this individual who has experienced bullying and discrimination at all stages of childhood and early adulthood. How might this affect Simeon's judgement in this scenario?

These practical, personal and organisational factors will all affect the quality of the analysis and subsequent decision-making and intervention (Wilkins and Boahen, 2013). There are various things that could counter these and aid a more critical analysis of the situation. These include, but are not limited to: research and more data gathering; reflective supervision; self-education and reflexive practice; and application of relevant law, policy and good practice guidance to Jasmine's situation.

> ### Danger point: applying theory uncritically
>
> As with every theory or model you use, ecological systems theory has its limitations. For example, while applying EST to a particular situation might help you to understand what is happening (a theory to inform), it does not always help to guide your decision-making or intervention (a theory to intervene) (Collingwood, 2005). While Seamus may have to cease transporting Jasmine, there may be no other alternatives available and Jasmine might not yet be ready to undertake that early morning journey alone. In terms of support from Simeon's social work agency, there might be no financial resources to help with transport costs, or the policy might not cover this particular situation (which is a constraint operating in Jasmine's mesosystem). This agency constraint effectively serves to undermine the possibility for good practice for Simeon. Pinpointing the real problem (the decision made by Seamus's employer) was straightforward in this scenario, but in real life it can be very tricky to unpick and isolate problematic interactions and relationships. Finally, when working with individuals and relationships, it is easy to neglect influencing factors in the macrosystem that are less tangible (such as gender systems, or societal beliefs and norms).

Why is critical analysis so important, and what skills are central to its success?

In addition to an understanding of what critical analysis actually is, it is important that you explicitly recognise the value of this in everyday social work practice, and we have alluded to some of the benefits of this above. The role and timing of critical analysis mean that it can be misconstrued and misrepresented as something that is done once you have gathered all the data that you need to make sense of a referral or situation. It is not. Analysis starts at the point at which you start thinking about the data in a referral or at the point at which you intervene with an individual or family. For instance, when you receive referral information, some level of analysis takes place that informs what you do next. Analysis is an ongoing process (in the same way that assessment is a process, not an event). There are, however, certain junctures where you have to be able to articulate your analysis (for example, during supervision discussions, or when writing a report).

Effective critical analysis enhances your decision-making, enables appropriate interventions, enables a responsive and flexible approach to working with people, and facilitates better case management. Effective critical analysis is reliant on various skills, including: time management and the ability to prioritise; organisational skills; cognitive skills (see Chapter 6); and a research mindset (see Chapter 5). The critical application of knowledge is a skill that relates to the last point (in terms of using research and other forms of knowledge, such as theory, in your analysis), and it is vital as you are able to select the appropriate type of knowledge and use it judiciously (bearing in mind its value and weaknesses – described in two case studies above and below which illustrate the application of theory).

Sound communication skills are vital too as you will need to spend a lot of time collecting information from people, carers, other family members and a wide range of professionals. The ability to communicate with different people goes hand-in-hand with having a good level of emotional intelligence. Emotional intelligence is the ability to recognise your own emotions as well as those of others (Howe, 2008). It is the ability to discern between different feelings and to identify and manage these in order to guide your thinking and behavioural responses. This is important in terms of managing the emotions in particular contexts and can be the difference between a successful intervention/good outcome, and one that is less so. Furthermore, these 'skills' (communication and emotional intelligence) are rooted to reflective practice and reflexivity (see Chapters 4 and 8).

Countering risk: looking for strengths

An alternative to praxis which is overly occupied with the identification and control of risk is the adoption of a strengths-based approach (Saleebey, 2013). Saleebey argues that this approach is a perspective, rather than a theory or model, which encourages social workers to use a lens which identifies strengths, not risks and deficits. In this way, a strengths-based approach can be used alongside other models for practice and can be a central part of the process of engaging in a critical analysis. Some of the underpinning principles of strengths-based thinking are as follows:

- Strengths and resources can be found in every individual, family, group and community.
- Avoid assumptions about the limits of a person, family, group or community to grow and change.
- Social work is about care, care-taking and hope (not risk management and control).
- Best practice is collaborative practice. (Saleebey, 2013: 17–21)

An additional principle is that trauma, abuse and adversity may cause harm, but they may also be sources of strength and opportunity. Thinking in this way takes a little more effort, involving critical thinking skills in order to identify those strengths and opportunities (see Box 7.5 for a case example). A benefit of strengths-based work is that it helps to address the power imbalance that is inherent in the social worker–service user relationship as it inevitably incorporates elements of empowering practice and partnership working. It does so by positioning the person you are working with as a 'problem-solver' rather than as the source of a problem (Rogers et al., 2016: 192). In the process of gathering information, questioning has a positive slant, rather than an overly negative focus on what has gone wrong. Therefore, a strength-based approach draws on specific types of questions such as:

Survival questions. In the past, how have you coped? What has previously worked in order for you to manage this problem/situation?

Support questions. Who gives you support and guidance? Where are they? Can you still access them if you need support?

Perspective questions. What do you think about the situation?

Esteem questions. What do people say about you that is positive? What do you like about yourself? What achievements are you proud of?

Value questions. What do you value in life?

Change questions. If you could change something in your life, what would it be? What help would you need to make this change?

It is not a case of negating or ignoring the information that you have in terms of the presenting problem and identified risks. The skill lies in combining different information and approaches to obtain a more balanced model for practice which can manage the risks while also working in a more empowering, strengths-based way, where possible.

 Box 7.6   Case study

The Hall/Jones family

On questioning Deena further in relation to how she acquired a black eye, Deena finally admits that this did result from conflict with her partner, Joe. Her injury was not the direct result of a physical assault, however. After Joe had returned home from the pub (where he had watched the match), Deena and Joe had got into an argument about money and the amount he had just spent on alcohol. Deena's daughter, Chantal, came in from the kitchen crying and shouting at them to stop. Chantal then threw the television remote at Deena and caused the injury. This was completely out of character for Chantal, who was a quiet, shy child. When the situation had calmed down, Deena tried to speak to Chantal, who refused to talk.

(Continued)

(Continued)

You speak to Chantal, who confides that she was worried that the argument between her mother and step-father, Joe, was going to get violent. She acted out of character and does not know why. Chantal had been very worried that she was going to get into trouble for hurting her mother and feeling guilty, convinced that she was a bad child. Social care services had originally become involved with the family because of concerns about domestic abuse, but also because of reports from school about Logan's presentation and the possibility of neglect. There had not been any concerns about Chantal other than that of living in a house where domestic abuse was present.

A strengths-based perspective in your work with Chantal might involve using some of the questioning techniques outlined above. These will help to engage Chantal and facilitate a conversation which is centred on her, and not her family's problems. At the same time, this would help to identify previous coping strategies and to work out why Chantal responded in the way she did during this more recent event. This could be helpful to Chantal in reminding her of how she previously coped and would help her to rid herself of the guilt about the incident.

Stop and reflect:

- Would you consider the conflict described above as an incident of domestic abuse? If yes, why? It not, why not?
- Whether or not you consider the situation described above to be classed as domestic abuse, why might Chantal have acted in the way that she did? How do you think she felt at that time?
- Why did Deena not tell you what had happened straight away? Is there any further work that you could do in relation to this?
- Think about the additional information that you might gather in your conversations with Chantal. How you might make sense of it? Revisit Chapter 2 on critical knowledge.
- Is there any further work that you could do with the family? Review Chapter 6 on professional judgement and decision-making.
- Do you need to focus on the continuing risks of domestic abuse or could you work in a strengths-based way with the whole family? If yes, how and with whom? If not, why not?

These questions are intended to assist a critical analysis of the presenting situation and the outcomes that you wish to achieve. Being clear about outcomes is an essential part of engaging in good critical analysis (Wilkins and Boahen, 2013). This is not limited to the outcomes that you wish for, but also includes the wishes and feelings of Chantal, Deena, Joe and Logan. Your analysis of the desired outcomes will likely raise some tensions, contradictions and, possibly, some ethical issues. Interrogating these forms part of your extended critical analysis.

Tools for analysis

So far in this chapter we have introduced you to various aspects of critical analysis such as the ability to use different forms of knowledge as well as various skills that are integral to the analytic process. In addition, there are some well-used tools that can be of value as part of your practitioner's toolkit and which can also be used in reflective, or reflexive, processes (see also Chapters 5 and 8).

SWOT/SCOR analysis

A SWOT analysis can be used in all kinds of scenarios and is not bound to any one particular discipline. Employing a SWOT analysis requires you to identify and consider strengths (S), weaknesses (W), opportunities (O) and threats (T) in any given situation. A slight adaptation enables the tool to be tailored towards social work: replacing the 'W' with 'C' to acknowledge challenges, and the 'T' with 'R' to represent risk/need (Dalzell and Sawyer, 2011). Table 7.1 displays the start of a worked example for the Hall/Jones family, with some details pertaining to Deena and Joe; can you add any more, and what would you include in a SCOR analysis for each child?

Danger point: applying theory uncritically

As with ecological systems theory (and all other theories and models), you should never use a model or perspective uncritically, that is, without being mindful of its limitations. So, what could be the limitations of using a strengths-based perspective? Safeguarding and other protective action might need to be the primary intervention, and it may not be possible to use a strengths-based approach if you are removing a child or using mental health legislation to hospitalise someone against their wishes. In addition, combining a strengths-based lens with other theories or models is skilled work and you may not have the confidence to approach direct work in this way, especially if there are particular concerns that must be taken seriously. Finally, as with all interventions, usually there is a resource implication to implementing plans or moving forward; there may not be the resources available to support a strengths-based piece of work.

Table 7.1   SCOR and the Hall/Jones family

Strengths	Challenges
• Deena has engaged with outreach support from a domestic abuse charity and wishes to attend their weekly women's group • Joe has started a domestic abuse perpetrator programme, with full attendance so far • Deena and Joe have openly said that they love each other and are committed to working to keep their family together	• Deena's travel arrangements to the women's group (in terms of cost, timing in relation to school, etc.) • Joe has been offered work over the summer – potential clash with the perpetrator programme

Opportunities	Risks/needs
• The house next door is available to rent – Deena's sister? • Perpetrator programmes often run outside of the working day – explore this	• Domestic abuse is an ongoing risk • Deena has had mental health problems in the past • Deena feels isolated • Joe finishing the perpetrator programme

Critical incident analysis

Another useful tool is the critical incident analysis (CIA) technique. Since the onset of the twentieth century, CIA techniques have increasingly been used in the fields of health, education, social care and social work. The role of CIA in these fields has been influenced by the work of Tripp (1993) who noted that:

> The vast majority of critical incidents ... are not at all dramatic or obvious: they are straightforward accounts of very commonplace events that occur in routine professional practice which are critical in the rather different sense that they are indicative of underlying trends, motives and structures. These incidents appear to be 'typical' rather than 'critical' at first sight but are rendered critical through analysis. (Tripp, 1993: 24–25)

In social work, this tool can help you to record and reflect on your everyday practice, providing a means of reflecting with your practice educator or line manager in order to engage in a reflective dialogue (Lister and Crisp, 2007). Undertaking CIA will help you to move beyond description and surface analysis to engage in a deeper level of understanding, analysis and more rounded conclusions. In accordance with Tripp's definition, the incident does not have to be a major event, or even a lengthy episode; it can be a brief encounter or intervention, as the value of undertaking a CIA lies in the depth of your analysis and contemplation. As such, this tool will help your developing critical thinking skills. As with many tools that require reflection and analysis, using a CIA framework requires an event or intervention to be more holistically scrutinised. This involves applying theory to understand the incident and consider theories and social work models to intervene, as well as prompting a more reflexive analysis of the impact of values, beliefs and other influences, such as agency policy (Lister and Crisp, 2007). A framework for CIA is set out in Box 7.7.

 **Box 7.7 Key point**

A critical incident analysis framework (adapted from Lister and Crisp, 2007: 49–50)

1. Account of the incident

    What happened? Where and when did it happen? Who was involved? What was your role and involvement in the incident? What was the focus and purpose of your involvement?

    What was the context of this incident? For instance, had you or your agency previously been involved with the individual or family?

2. Initial responses to the incident

    What were your initial thoughts and feelings at the time?

    What were the responses of other relevant individuals to this incident? If unknown, can you think what these might have been?

3. Issues and dilemmas highlighted by this incident

    What dilemmas for practice were recognised in light of this incident?

    What are the ethical issues highlighted by this incident?

    What values are acknowledged in relation to this incident?

    Are there any inter-agency implications highlighted as a result of this incident?

4. Learning

    What have you learned from your involvement in this incident, for example, in relation to your sense of self, relationships with others, social work activity and your own practice, organisational policy and protocols?

    What theories have helped, or might have helped, to develop your understanding in relation to the incident?

    What research helped, or might have helped, to develop your understanding in relation to the incident?

    What legislation and/or organisational policy help to understand or underpin aspects of the incident?

    What future learning can you identify as a result of your involvement in this incident?

5. Outcomes

    Reflect on the various participants. What were the outcomes following this incident?

    What are your thoughts and feelings about the incident now?

    Are there any particular ways in which this incident has led to a change in how you think, feel or will act in future situations?

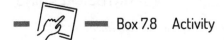 ▬ Box 7.8 Activity ▬▬▬▬▬▬▬▬▬▬▬▬▬▬▬

Serious case reviews and critical incident analyses

Now you understand the use and functioning of a CIA, you should review some published serious case reviews or public inquiry reports. Try to identify how the principles of CIA have been applied in the undertaking of the review. Is there some identified learning from the findings of the review? This learning should inform and improve practice (not only for social work but also for allied professions such as health or the police).

SUMMARY

In this chapter we have focused on critical thinking in an applied way, highlighting the centrality of critical analysis in practice. We have done so by identifying the nature of social work activity in relation to our work with both risks and strengths. In addition, we have underlined the importance of viewing risk through both a negative and positive lens by illuminating the value of positive risk-taking in enabling people to engage in processes of validation, resilience and skills building. This chapter has also introduced two important theories for social work – ecological systems theory and a strengths-based approach (Bronfenbrenner, 1979; Saleebey, 2013). These have been applied to a case study to illustrate the ways in which theory and practice meet. This is an aspect of practice which has been maligned in the past, with claims that practitioners do not need theory in the 'real world', or that there is no time for theorising. Both are untrue, and you will knowingly and unknowingly use theory throughout your practice life to assist your understanding of events, individuals and families as well as to guide your practice decisions. Finally, this chapter has introduced you to two very different tools which are underpinned by critical analytical skills to help you to see how there are techniques to help your developing skills in critical analysis.

Having read this chapter, you should be able to articulate:

- What is meant by critical analysis
- The understanding that critical analysis is not a one-off activity, but should form part of your mindset in social work practice
- An eclectic approach which combines working with risk (the bread and butter of social work) and employing a strengths-based perspective
- Different tools that rely upon critical analysis.

FURTHER READING

Rutter, L. and Brown, K. (2015). *Critical Thinking and Professional Judgement for Social Work*. London: Learning Matters.

Staempfli, A., Adshead., L. and Fletcher, J. (2015). Ready for qualified practice? A comparative study of capability for critical reflection and analysis of MA Social Work and MA Step Up to Social Work students at the end of second placement. *Social Work Education*, 34(8), 952–966.

Wilkins, D. and Boahen, G. (2013). *Critical Analysis Skills for Social Workers*. Maidenhead: Open University Press.

8

REFLEXIVITY AND THE USE OF SELF

Introduction

In Chapter 5 we introduced you to the concept of reflection *in* and *on* practice. In this chapter, we introduce you to the concept of reflexivity and explain why reflexive practice is an essential activity that enables you to reflect *before* practice, thus closing the loop on reflection and cementing your knowledge, values and skills as you move from being an intuitive reflector to a critical reflector. By engaging in reflexive practice, we hope that you will seek to balance a sensitive awareness of your own knowledge, thoughts and feelings with the views and perceptions of others before, during and after each example of work that you complete.

Considering the dangers of intuitive practice that overlooks or minimises the need to assess, analyse and evaluate verifiable evidence, we will explain why effective, safe and competent practice requires a sensitive, honest and accurate awareness of your own knowledge, thoughts and feelings. But even more than this, reflexivity requires you to contextualise this knowledge of the self alongside the views and perceptions of others. Focusing on your developing practice wisdom, we will explain why a sustained approach to reflexive practice should enable you to constantly think about how you can influence and affect the experiences of and outcomes for those people you are working to support. Recognising your primary aim to continually improve practices and outcomes for people and their communities, we will highlight some opportunities and strategies so that you can consider reducing the impact of your own personal values, knowledge, skills, attitudes, communication styles and prejudices on your ability to assess and analyse the lived experiences of others effectively and credibly.

Social work as a form of surveillance?

A common thread that runs through this book is the need for social workers to constantly think about how social work practices are affecting the experiences of and outcomes for people being supported. Indeed, the social worker's goal to continually improve practices and outcomes for people and their communities is a key message contained in each chapter. One of the greatest challenges to improve practice and, in turn, the outcomes of the people you are working to support is that social work is often perceived as an invasion of people's right to private family life. This is because social work is a representative layer of governmentality, one of the positions that radical social work seeks to undo.

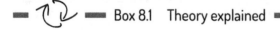 **Box 8.1   Theory explained**

Governmentality is a term used to describe the way that social work contributes to the political mission to construct and maintain a harmonious society. The pursuit of a harmonious society, however, comes at a price. In relation to this book and the task of social work practice, the price is seen in a society that views some people as being harmonious and others as not. While social workers are predominantly orientated towards facilitating opportunities for individuals, families and communities to experience a harmonious society, it must be recognised that this work forms part of a wider set of coordinated state-sponsored activities. So long as social work remains a publicly funded endeavour, the government will determine what a social worker does and what they will not do. As an apparatus of state control, social work and social workers will often be viewed by those people you are training to support as a form of government surveillance.

The opportunity for social workers to become involved in the private family lives of others, whether invited or not, means that conflict can become a defining characteristic of any professional relationship. Sometimes this conflict will be obvious, sometimes it will not. What you must try to avoid is blaming individuals for their reaction to your involvement.

You will often become involved in the lives of others where there are concerns about risk, vulnerability, capacity or resilience. The nature of your involvement would be to assess the situation (see Chapters 6 and 7) and then make a professional judgement, ideally in collaboration with the people you are training to support, about what steps need to be taken to reduce risk or vulnerability and to promote capacity and resilience. Of equal importance is the need for you to monitor progress so that you can measure how successful your facilitation of any change might be. At all times, you must try to be 'reflexive' so that your involvement in the lives of others, the work you are required to do and the outcomes you agree, are considered since the work that you do could be characterised by suspicion and fear and sometimes conflict.

▬ 🔄 ▬ Box 8.2   Theory explained ▬▬▬▬▬▬▬▬▬▬▬▬▬

According to Fook and Askeland (2006), *reflexivity* is a term used in social work to describe three essential elements of practice. First, it is used to refer to the way that social work seeks to understand what life is like through the eyes of those people who social workers are working to support. Second, it is defined as a social worker's ability to critically reflect on the evidence that has been gathered about the people you are training to support and how this knowledge is used to justify projects of both care and control. Third, reflexivity is concerned with the need to avoid emotive decision-making. Together they provide a platform from which to turn a mirror on social work practice so that the principles of governmentality can be understood in pursuit of a more democratic process.

Effective methods to achieve reflexivity, and the need to avoid blaming people for their reaction to you, first require you to understand what you bring to the working relationship in terms of attitudes and beliefs. Here, ethical and effective social work practice demands specific efforts to isolate presuppositions and to consider how any stereotypes, pre-judgements and biases may influence or undermine the legitimacy of social work. However, while the traditional approach to practice draws heavily on the expectation that you will reflect 'on' and 'in' practice, the value of reflexivity, the skill to reflect before action, as a method to achieve the critical reflection status discussed in Chapter 4, has not been fully explored in the social work literature.

Let us now consider the importance of reflexivity through the following case study.

 Box 8.3   Case study

Jonathan is working to support a young woman called Selda. Selda is from Syria. She is 14 and is living with the label 'asylum seeker'.

Jonathan is not from Syria. He is from Cardiff. He is a 37-year-old social work student. He lives in a three-bedroom house in the leafy suburbs with his partner and two children. For many years, Jonathan has worked in an assertive outreach team as a support worker. He sees his future social work career in adult mental health services. Jonathan is on placement in a charitable organisation that works to support people living with the label 'asylum seeker'. He likes the placement but often complains to his peers that he feels frustrated because he never gets the opportunity to do proper social work.

Jonathan has been asked by a social worker to meet Selda, for the first time, as an advocate. He has been asked to talk to her about her situation and the residential children's home that she is currently living in. Given his experience of working within an assertive outreach team, Jonathan feels that he does not need to prepare for the meeting with Selda. He thinks that this visit will be easy, because this work is not proper social work.

Questions:

1.   Why might Jonathan's initial thoughts and feelings be wrong?
2.   What preparation might Jonathan need?

This is a difficult case study because there are so many factors that need to be considered. Let us start with governmentality.

Selda is from Syria. She is 14 and is living with the label 'asylum seeker'. Why is this information important? Well, we should know that in Syria, at the time of writing, a war rages on. People are fleeing the country in massive numbers, seeking any opportunity to escape the violence that they have witnessed. Desperate for a better life, victims of war, some of whom have experienced torture, rape, grief, separation and loss, dispossession, displacement and the complete annihilation of families, communities and the basic human rights that we all take for granted, often pay human traffickers to bring them to a place of safety. Some are even abducted by human traffickers and taken to Europe for labour or sexual exploitation. In many countries throughout the world, the soldiers who kill, the corrupt political actors who incite violence, the police and the public officials who advocate violence are all engaged in state-sponsored activities of aggression – the same aggression that helpless people like Selda are attempting to flee.

The journey to a safe European home for many people fleeing persecution and abuse is treacherous. Those who have the money often pay thousands of pounds to a human trafficker who promises a prosperous future, before being forced onto small unseaworthy boats and driven across hundreds of miles of ocean. The lucky ones make landfall. Others are abandoned to their own defences, often stranded off the European coast while government officials bicker about the worth of human life, and why they should continue to shoulder the responsibility for a humanitarian crisis caused by other government officials.

If those people fleeing persecution and abuse make landfall, they are treated as criminals. Often detained in modern-day concentration camps or left to fend for themselves, they remain vulnerable to violence, exploitation and terror as they make their own way north or, like Selda, are transported north as a part of an intergovernmental immigration scheme.

Those young people who arrive in the UK without parents, like Selda, are entitled to the same rights as other 'looked-after' children and young people. This includes accommodation, some finance, education, statutory health assessments, support and care plan reviews. Most of the young people who arrive in the UK and who live with the label 'asylum seeker' will be given discretionary leave to remain until they are 17½ years old, leaving the detailed processing of an asylum application for when they are older, when they may or may not be given indefinite leave to remain if their status changes to mean that they are living with the label 'refugee'. The sense of isolation, uncertainty and insecurity often compounds unresolved trauma as young people living with the label 'asylum seeker', just like Selda, become distressed as they try to understand their new school, their new home, their new country.

Despite this distress, those living with the label 'asylum seeker' or 'refugee' continue to be persecuted by a political system that encourages anti-immigration policies. For many young people living with the label 'asylum seeker' or 'refugee', Islamophobia makes them consistent targets of hate. They are ridiculed, bullied and vilified by those who view immigration as a threat to the 'harmonious' nature of society. This antipathy has far-reaching effects in society that even reach social work students, like Jonathan, who lives in the leafy suburbs in a cosy three-bedroom house, content in the arrogant belief that they know the difference between what social work is and what social work is not, and on this basis fail to prepare to meet some of the most vulnerable young people in society, like Selda.

If this example is coming across as extreme, we want to you think about who you are and the people you are studying social work with. As social work is a protected activity in the UK, requiring education to degree level so that you can facilitate change and the emancipation of others, there is an awkward fact that many of the people you are training to support can only dream about the opportunity of studying for a degree. Not only do you enjoy the opportunity and privilege of a degree in social work but you will be paid to intervene in the lives of others to facilitate change in the pursuit of improved outcomes. You will enjoy the privilege to be paid to work with people who might not usually invite you into their lives. You will use your (super)powers to assess, plan and implement programmes of support that you recommend based upon your own knowledge, values and skills. But before you do this, we want you to think about your proximity to those whose lives are limited and often curtailed by chronic structural discrimination and inequality – those who are homeless, those who cannot afford to eat every day, those who cannot afford to heat their homes, those who are judged and criticised by society for being different, those who are labelled as representing a threat to the harmony of society. We want you to think about the reasons why you have a right to be involved in people's lives, even if you are not invited. We want you to think about your proximity to the people you are training to support, and your ability to see the world through their eyes. Because that skill presents the first essential step to achieving reflexivity in your social work practice. Does that still sound extreme?

Reflexivity, a skill lacking in the above case study, requires you to consciously consider how your personal beliefs and values, assumptions, family imprinting and cultural conditioning impact on your approach to practice. As you build the necessary skills needed to become critically reflective, you should also become determined to democratise social work practice and value the inclusion of experts by experience in all social work activities. If this summary of the discussion so far is complicated, try not to worry. We will now explore the possible opportunities for you to achieve these approaches.

How to become a reflexive practitioner

One of the first steps to reflexivity, and the opportunity to become reflexive, requires you to turn a mirror in on yourself. It requires you to understand how you see yourself, not as the personal you relaxing at home, but as the social worker you. At some point in the future (and hopefully by graduation), the personal you and the professional social worker you will merge. You will be a social worker relaxing at home in the same way that you will be a social worker conducting an assessment. There should be no light to shine between the personal and professional you. For some, this merger may well have already happened.

The second step to reflexivity requires you to imagine how the people you are training to support see you and to accept, if you are unable to understand, that what you see and what they see may be quite different. To start off on this journey, try to turn the mirror in on yourself by engaging, as fully as you are able, in the three exercises in Box 8.4.

— 🖼 — Box 8.4   Activity ═══════════════════════════

Exercise 1. Imagine that you are standing in front of a mirror. What do you see? Do you see a gender, a religion, a sexuality? Do you see height, weight, eye colour, hair colour, skin colour? Do you see someone who is sociable, or do you see somebody who is shy? Do you see someone who is confident, or do you see someone who lacks skill? Do you see a father, a mother, a sister, a brother, a daughter, a son? Do you see somebody you are proud of? Try to spend some quiet reflection time being mindful of your own reflection.

Exercise 2. Now consider the case study in Box 8.3. Spend some quiet reflection time being mindful about the things that you think Selda might see when she looks at Jonathan for the very first time. Do you think that Jonathan would be happy with her initial impression?

Exercise 3. Imagine that you have been asked to visit Selda to talk to her about her situation and the residential children's home that she is currently living in. What do you think she might see when she looks at you?

By turning a mirror in on yourself and imagining how you are perceived by the people you are training to support, reflexivity becomes a circular process whereby you can begin to make sense of the potential difference between cause and effect. A reflexive relationship in social work is therefore bidirectional, with both cause and consequence affecting one another in a relationship which neither you nor the person you are working to support might be aware of (Allen, 2018). More than this, though, reflexivity enables you to complete the circle of reflection where you can critically examine your approaches to practice before action as well as in and on action.

The main challenge to reflection on action, using such models as described in Chapter 4, is that there is a tendency for arrogance at one extreme of the reflection scale, whereby you feel that no improvement is needed in your practice because the skills you have are second to none. At the other end of the scale is the impostor syndrome (Allen and Riding, 2018), where you are unable to think positively at all as you question the reasons why you are on the course and why you have been let loose to work with others. Hopefully, you can see why both reactions to reflection are problematic but finding the middle ground can be difficult, particularly if you are on placement and do not protect the valuable time in the day that is set aside for reflection. It can be all too easy to reschedule reflection time, the time to sit quietly to contemplate your approaches to practice, if others around you are rushing around doing what you perceive to be 'proper social work'. This is one of the reasons why reflexivity is essential. Not only does it create an opportunity for you to think about the potential impact that you might have on the people you are training to support, but it also starts the reflective cycle off much sooner in the action process.

Completing a critical reflection cycle

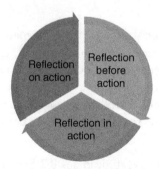

Figure 8.1 Critical reflection cycle

If used effectively, reflection before action can enable you to consider how the broader social perception of you as a social worker, an agent of the state working to address social discord in pursuit of a political ambition for a harmonious society, can be exceptionally helpful – most notably because you may begin to consider the people you are training to support in the context of those structural discriminatory factors that operate around them. A sensitive awareness of racism, sexism, homophobia, restrained opportunities for social mobility and social justice, ageism and an understanding of a person's lived experience of trauma and oppression can bring you closer to some of the realities that you have little experience of yourself. Of course, as you develop your practice wisdom you will be able to trust these considerations, but then verify the same through the conversations that you have.

Reflection before action

According to heuristic and phenomenological paradigms (another word for 'theory') that arguably underpin reflexive approaches, any systematic approach to 'reflection before action' must have as its explicit focus a recognised need to uncover and challenge the power dynamics that frame practice. Pre-reflection must be used to uncover and analyse stereotypical assumptions or pre-judgements that you might have about the people you are training to support and the situations in which they live.

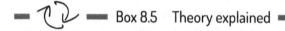

Box 8.5   Theory explained

Heuristic social work is a theoretical principle that describes how you, and the people who you are training to support, solve problems and make judgements quickly and efficiently. Intuition can shorten decision-making time and allow people to function without constantly stopping to think about their next course of action. Heuristics are helpful in many situations, but they can also lead to biases if perceptions or intuitions are not accurate or verifiable. What social work theories and methods do you think align with heuristic social work?

Phenomenology is the study of structures of consciousness as experienced from the first-person point of view. The central structure of phenomenology is the focus on another's lived experience and the meaning that individuals attribute to it. What social work theories and methods do you think align with phenomenology?

In a media-dominated society, those who are seen to create social discord (those living with an enduring mental health difficulty, those who are unemployed, obese or addicted to substances, those who are elderly, those who are in prison, those who rely on state benefits and those people who seek asylum and refuge in another country to experience the same human rights that you and I may take for granted) are often portrayed as being different. This public perception, if you are not careful, can contaminate your perceptions, highlighting a path to confirmation bias. If an individual, family or community is frequently labelled as being different for creating social discord and not conforming to a wider political vision of social harmony, whatever that may be, social workers can confirm that position through the application of reflected action. Just as Jonathan dismissed the valuable work he was asked to do with Selda, you too might dismiss the need to work with some people whom society has written off as a lost cause.

Danger point: taking people as you find them

When talking about the importance of reflexivity in class, some students say that they always take people as they find them. They would never pre-judge because they treat each person they work with in the same way. While this approach may be useful in private, it becomes problematic in social work because this approach will rarely be reciprocated. Some of the people you work to support will perceive you as a threat. For this reason, we suggest that students might do well to revise their position. While we respect the principle of reserved judgement, we know that equality does not mean treating all people in the same way. Given the sensitive nature of our work, we know that social workers must take into account how they will be perceived before meeting a person for the first time. We must be sensitive to a person's lived experiences, previous encounters with social workers, personal characteristics and position within society. It is important not to judge people before meeting them, but it is important to judge the way that you may be perceived so that you can prepare and act to reduce any potential fear and suspicion. This approach is essential as you will certainly have to work differently with survivors of abuse and perpetrators of abuse. Turn the mirror in on yourself – what do you want the different people you work with to see according to their own particular context?

Finding the opportunity to reflect before action is, therefore, the first stage in reflexive practice. Used effectively, 'reflection before action' could help you to acknowledge the fact that all the relationships that you seek to develop with people over the course of your career might be fixed within historical, social and political dynamics which have served to construct boundary distinctions such as fear and mistrust between social workers and those people who receive social work support. In some situations, the relationships that you seek to develop may, at least initially, be characterised by suspicion and fear (including your own), and this can only be dealt with if it is first acknowledged.

Arguably, the most important need for reflexivity and the need to reflect before action can be found on those occasions when you are meeting somebody for the first time, and on other occasions where you may have to deliver bad news or challenge the views of another professional. The feelings that accompany these events are likely to be personal and might differ from person to person, but to consider a strategy for reflexivity you are invited to test the 'six-minute social worker'. This model has been devised by Allen (2018), and it is so-called because he believes it usually takes a practised and confident social worker about six minutes to complete (see Box 8.6). Do not worry if it takes you a little longer.

 **Box 8.6   Activity**

Reflection before action using the 'six-minute social worker' model

Try to recall an experience on placement where you were asked to meet somebody for the first time. If you have not been on placement yet, imagine a situation where you have been asked to meet somebody as a social work student. Once you have an example, follow the six steps below:

Step 1. Start by writing a list of those words or phrases which best describe how you might be feeling and what you might be thinking about working with this individual/ family/community.

Step 2. Read over the list of words or phrases and reflect on the way that these thoughts and feelings might impact on your social work practice.

Step 3. Write down a strategy that might enable you to put these thoughts and feelings to one side so that they do not impact on your professional behaviour.

Step 4. Using your sociological imagination, write a list of words or phrases to describe how the individual/family/community might be feeling and what they might be thinking about you.

Step 5. Read over this second list of words or phrases and reflect on how these thoughts and feelings might impact on your social work practice.

Step 6. Using the information gathered so far, reflect on the theories, methods and layers of support that you might need to form an effective working alliance and to achieve mutually satisfactory solutions.

Within the planning stage of social work practice (stage 6 of the six-minute social worker model in Box 8.6), you should seek to develop a series of conversation starters that ask individuals, families and communities to tell you what they want or need to improve their situation, and ultimately move to a position of independence when social worker involvement is no longer required. This is particularly important as you locate yourself as a facilitator of change that requires honesty and cooperation and the need to build trusting and valued partnerships.

A core social work skill needed to achieve this requires you to ensure that the people you are working to support understand and recognise that they

Danger point

- Do not overlook the value of reflection before action. Always try to make time for it.
- Do not suppress or ignore feelings of anxiety or distress. Identify them, externalise them by writing them down and talk about them in supervision.
- Do not underestimate the impact of your personal beliefs and values, assumptions, family imprinting and cultural conditioning on your approach to practice.
- Do not overlook the need to verify social work philosophical ideologies and practices with the support of experts by experience.
- Try to ensure that all your reflection before, in and on practice is primarily concerned with promoting the democratic ideals of social work.

have a voice, and that their voice is being heard. Turnell and Edwards (1999) and Turnell and Essex (2006) show, for instance in the application of Signs of Safety®, how social workers can help people to focus their concerns by enabling them to realise their own opportunities, strengths and fears. In line with the concept of reflexivity, this approach to enablement could be demonstrated when working with others in statements such as 'I can hear that you do not want me to interfere in your life. It must be very hard for you to accept me being involved in your family, given that you do not like it.' As Ferguson (2011) explains, this open dialogue can then pave the way for you to provide the people you are training to support with an objective: 'It is very important that I work with you and your family. How can we work together in a productive way so that I do not need to be involved in your family any more?'

Seeking objectives that reflect the principles described in Chapter 4, the validation of others' concerns and the pursuit of co-produced solutions can create an opportunity for you to reduce conflict and the possibility that your involvement will be perceived as state interference. As a useful method in the social work assessment, this style of questioning can prove invaluable when applied strategically in a carefully considered conversation (Ferguson, 2011).

Consistent with the need to trust and verify, meaningful attempts should be made to verify hypothetical responses, or seek alternative responses, through more direct and deliberate forms of procedural, questioning and exchange models of assessment. To be reflexive, this approach should always major in lived experience and focus strategically and systematically on the individual's strengths, weaknesses, opportunities and threats as encountered or projected.

Danger point

The importance of selecting hypothetical questions as a strategy in assessment and continuing safe social work practice does, however, raise some concerns regarding the need to exercise a degree of sensitivity. A hypothetical question can only really be answered with a hypothetical response. As such, some people may perceive hypothetical questions with a degree of suspicion as they require a degree of imagination that may otherwise be seen as unusual. Summarising the results of a study which aimed to examine concepts of health, Currer (1986) found that the method of asking women of Pathan decent to consider whether their life might be enhanced by being 'in someone else's shoes' created a sense of misunderstanding. She found that asking these women to consider a response to this hypothetical question became problematic as each person considered their place on earth, the shoes that they were in, to have been given to them by Allah. As such, they found any attempt to consider an alternative position, what life might be like if they were in someone else's shoes, to be at odds with their cultural and religious beliefs.

By engaging children, families and communities so as to allow them to discuss their strengths, weaknesses, opportunities and threats using both hypothetical and more direct forms of questioning, you may apply reflexive practice to challenge governmentality, thus demonstrating that intervention is based on the praxis of equity and inclusive respect. With a principle of equality laid out, you should be better positioned to explain that you are only involved in a person's life because there are significant concerns about risk, capacity or vulnerability – not because a person may be perceived by society as being different. Let us now consider how Jonathan might have responded in his placement if he had adopted and applied the concept of reflexivity.

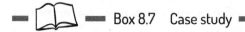 Box 8.7   Case study

Jonathan is working to support a young woman called Selda. Selda is from Syria. She is 14 and is living with the label 'asylum seeker'.

Jonathan is not from Syria. He is from Cardiff. He is a 37-year-old social work student. He lives in a three-bedroom house in the leafy suburbs with his partner and two children. For many years, Jonathan has worked in an assertive outreach team as a support worker. He sees his future social work career in adult mental health services. Jonathan is on placement in a charitable organisation that works to support all people living with the label 'asylum seeker'. Given his previous experience in adult mental health services, Jonathan recognises that he has many practical skills that are transferable to this placement. He has done a lot of research on the asylum and refugee law and is often shocked when he speaks to people who use the placement as he hears about the adversity and trauma that they have faced in their lives. Jonathan feels lucky never to have experienced torture, abuse and human trafficking. He appreciates the fact that he has a safe home and that he and his family take their human rights for granted. Jonathan has read a wide range of research on trauma and child and adolescent mental health, but is worried about meeting Selda. He tries the six-minute social worker model to try to develop a strategy for the first meeting.

Step 1. Jonathan starts by writing a list of those words or phrases which best describe how he is feeling and what he is thinking about working with Selda. These are his responses:

- I am worried about meeting Selda because I am a man. I think Selda might benefit from a female worker
- I am nervous that I cannot speak her language. I think I might do well to find out what language Selda speaks so I can learn how to say hello and how to introduce myself
- I think that I will need an interpreter, but I am aware that a translator might cause Selda some distress if they are from Syria too
- I think Selda might find me intimidating because she might see me as an agent of the state
- I feel sorry for Selda
- I believe that Selda will not want to talk to me

Step 2. Jonathan reads over the list of words and phrases and reflects on the way that these thoughts and feelings might impact on his social work practice. These are his responses:

- If I am worried that I am not a suitable person to work with Selda, because I am a man, I might not engage as fully as I should
- Being nervous that I cannot speak Selda'a language, I act in a clumsy or ignorant way as I try to devise a mutually understandable communication system
- I might not include the interpreter or apologise for their presence
- Being aware that Selda might find me intimidating, I might apologise for my presence. I might not conduct a thorough assessment
- By feeling sorry for Selda I might patronise her.
- If I assume that she does not want to talk to me, I might end the meeting quickly if confirmation bias undermines my confidence even further

Step 3. Jonathan writes down a strategy that might enable him to put these thoughts and feelings to one side so that they do not impact on his professional behaviour:

- I need to speak to more experienced colleagues and ask for advice on how to manage the first meeting. I remember that it might be inappropriate to shake Selda's hand, for example, but need to verify this first
- I need to learn a few phrases, like 'As-salaam alaikum', to help demonstrate that I do not represent a threat. I also need to be mindful about what I am wearing and the need to speak quietly but with confidence
- I need to find out if an interpreter is required
- I need to ask for advice on where the best meeting place would be
- I need to learn the detail of immigration law and tell Selda that I am not there to send her back to Syria
- I need to be able to learn how best to tell her that I am her advocate

(Continued)

(Continued)

Step 4. Using his sociological imagination, Jonathan now writes a list of words or phrases to describe how Selda might be feeling and what she might be thinking about him:

- Worried
- Scared
- Confused
- Anxious
- Intimidated
- Panic

Step 5. Jonathan reads over this second list of words or phrases and reflects on how these thoughts and feelings might impact on his social work practice. This is his response:

- If I am worried and Selda is worried, we may never make any positive progress together
- Selda might not feel comfortable talking to me. She might hide her face or even refuse to meet me
- Selda might become aggressive if she sees me as a threat
- Selda might tell me things she thinks that I want to hear. She might not be honest about her situation
- Selda might not engage with the interpreter
- Selda might demonstrate a mental health difficulty

Step 6. Using the information gathered so far, Jonathan reflects on the theories, methods and layers of support that he might need to form an effective working alliance with Selda and to achieve mutually satisfactory solutions:

- Consistent with cognitive behavioural theory, I assume that my thoughts and feelings and Selda's thoughts and feelings might influence our behaviour. If our thoughts are changed, our behaviour will change. For this reason, before visiting Selda, I will write her a letter introducing myself and tell her the reasons why I am visiting. I will include a photo of myself and write about my favourite food and hobbies. I will ask a key worker at the residential home to read the letter to Selda ahead of the meeting to help her understand the reasons why I am going to see her.
- Using motivational interviewing techniques, I will prepare information and leaflets that I can give to Selda. These leaflets will explain her rights and the process of application for refugee status.
- Applying a person-centred approach, I will seek advice from a more experienced colleague about how to demonstrate the principles of empathy, congruence and unconditional positive regard as necessary in the helping relationship.

- Using my knowledge of the recovery model, I will ask Selda if she would like to be part of the local peer support group where young people living with the label 'asylum seeker' or 'refugee' support other young people to share ideas and make sense of their own lived experiences.
- I will ask for advice regarding the interpreter and follow the actions that my onsite supervisors decide.
- Adopting narrative theory, I will prepare a question and exchange model of assessment that supports Selda to feel in control of her narrative and draw her attention, without promising anything, to the possibility of a different narrative for the future (the possibility of being safe).
- I will give Selda detailed information about whom to contact if she wishes to complain about me or any of the other people working to support her.

Questions:

1. Why might the approach to reflexive practice enable Jonathan to work more effectively with Selda?
2. What are the barriers to reflection before action?
3. What are the solutions needed to overcome these barriers?

SUMMARY

Learning how to become a reflexive practitioner requires you to turn the mirror in on your own social work practice so that you can begin to examine it and the historical, political and social context within which you operate. You must also consider how your position and identity will be viewed by those people you are training to support. If you imagine that you might be anxious when working with a person for the first time, and then imagine that they might be anxious too, you can begin to develop a strategy to reduce these thoughts and feelings during your social work intervention. Unless these thoughts and feelings are identified and considered, you may quickly come to blame the people you are training to support for 'disguised compliance' or worse.

Reflexivity is a fundamental skill that is difficult to master. It requires you to be honest with yourself, but at the same time apply emotional intelligence that is neither arrogant nor overly critical. Taking people as you find them may be perfectly natural in your private life, but in your professional life, and as the personal you and the social work you begin to merge, the need to consider the historical, political and social context of the people you are training to support, before you meet them for the first time, is very important, not least because they will view you from that perspective too.

Having read this chapter, you should be able to:

- Begin to recognise the context within which social work operates
- Understand that reflexivity is a key process that closes the critical reflection loop
- Value the need to view life through the eyes of the people you are working to support and adjust your practice accordingly
- Understand the importance of reflection before action
- Recognise that the people you are training to support might perceive you as an agent of the state
- Recognise how stereotypes and presuppositions could contaminate your practice.

FURTHER READING

Bourdieu, P. (1977). *Outline of a Theory of Practice*. Cambridge: Cambridge University Press.

Butler, A., Ford, D. and Tregaskis, C. (2007). Who do we think we are? Self and reflexivity in social work practice. *Qualitative Social Work*, 6(3), 281–299.

Ferguson, I. (2011). *Reclaiming Social Work: Challenging Neo-liberalism and Promoting Social Justice*. London: Sage.

9

ANALYTICAL ASSESSMENTS AND REPORT WRITING

.... THEORETICAL BACKGROUND

- Indigenous knowledge
- Theories of social work
- Team development

.... RELEVANCE TO SOCIAL WORK THINKING AND PRACTICE

- High-quality assessments
- Verifiable evidence
- Accountability
- Freedom of information

.... REAL-WORLD CHALLENGES

- Confirmation bias
- Judgemental attitudes
- Conflict in group dynamics

Introduction

Analysis is a core social work skill that requires a significant commitment to continual professional development and self-awareness. Highlighting the central importance of evidence-based and evidence-informed practice that draws on the **indigenous knowledge** of the people social work seeks to support, this chapter will consider the assessment process. We will include some practical guidance on barriers to completing analytical assessment and offer some tools and techniques to help you address issues of engagement, power, resistance and complexity.

Drawing together the themes that have been presented in the preceding chapters, we will further illustrate the complex nature of analysis and assessment. We will revisit the problematic concept of resistance and the label **'disguised compliance'** to provide a series of opportunities for you to consider social work as a management function that facilitates change through multi-agency working, engagement, enablement, power and disengagement.

Working in partnership to develop evidence-based practice

According to Sheppard et al. (2000), evidence-based practice is a process that requires you to combine well-researched interventions with your developing experience and ethics, and the preferences and culture of the people you are working to support, to guide and inform the delivery of services. It requires you to be an expert facilitator of conversations so that you can develop relationships with others that help support the process of change. In bringing together your knowledge of law, governance, theories, methods and ethics with the value of person-centred approaches to practice and the skills to form effective reflexive relationships with others, you may also be demonstrating your readiness for early-career status. But because social work is an activity with a purpose, it is important to remember that much of the work you do will be in response to a referral. You may be asked to investigate an allegation pertaining to risk, harm, vulnerability or capacity. You may also be asked to investigate concerns about a person's welfare, safety or daily living activities. Whatever the reason for social work intervention, you will be tasked with the responsibility of using evidence-based practice to underpin your investigation.

As an investigator, you are required to verify the information that you have been presented with. In most situations, this information will be provided to you from a referral, a complaint, a review process or a multi-agency team meeting. We will consider the composition of the multi-agency team, and the role of the people you are training to support within that shortly, but it is important that we spend some time considering the relationship between social work, evidence-based practice and indigenous knowledge further.

▬ 〰 ▬ Box 9.1   Theory explained ▬▬▬▬▬▬▬▬▬▬▬

Indigenous knowledge

In 2014, the International Federation of Social Workers approved the following definition of social work:

> Social work is a practice-based profession and an academic discipline that promotes social change and development, social cohesion, and the empowerment and liberation of people. Principles of social justice, human rights, collective responsibility and respect for diversities are central to social work. Underpinned by theories of social work, social sciences, humanities and indigenous knowledge, social work engages people and structures to address life challenges and enhance wellbeing.

However, the term 'indigenous knowledge' requires some clarification. In the context of the IFSW definition, indigenous knowledge is not meant to apply to the knowledge of indigenous people, but rather to the assumed fact that within each one of us there is an explanation or an interpretation of the world in which we live. If we associate the term 'indigenous knowledge' with the term 'expert by experience', for instance, we begin to see the similarity in the letter and spirit of exchange models of assessment discussed in Chapter 6. The task facing the social worker, however, is first to develop the relationship required to facilitate the opportunity for people to share their indigenous knowledge of the world in which they live so that the intricacies of their reality can be understood. As social workers attempt to see the world through the eyes of the people they are working to support, they must first establish their views, opinions, hopes, dreams and aspirations. They must be prepared to learn from the people they are working to support and use the 'indigenous knowledge' that they uncover to situate, confirm or refute the theories of social work, social sciences, humanities before enabling others to address life challenges and enhance wellbeing.

Focusing on indigenous knowledge requires the social worker to make a considered judgement about the quality, reliability and legitimacy of evidence – evidence that comes from primary and secondary sources (see Chapter 3) as well as the evidence that comes directly from the people you are training to support. Balancing the judgement about which source of evidence is most viable does not mean that one should take precedence over the other. Instead, each social work assessment or investigation should apply knowledge of social work theory, social sciences, humanities, biology and psychology alongside the knowledge of the individual expert by experience to critically reflect on the information available and analyse any situation, before synthesising meaning and agreeing on any course of action. But, in the same way that critical reflection is a skill that varies from one person to another, the ability to analyse, synthesise and work in partnership with others is something that needs practice too.

Most social work degree programmes facilitate opportunities for students to practise the application of their analytical skills in written assignments and dissertations. Others require social work students to complete a module on research. Yet, in our collective experience of lecturing on social work, we regularly meet students who do not value the relationship between doing social work practice and social work research. The fact that social work practice and social work research are almost identical – separated only by the fact that the people we interview for research must consent to our involvement whereas those we interview as part of our social work practice might not – is often misunderstood by students who are eager to be out of the classroom applying their knowledge in the real world. But, as a profession that seeks to gather, compile and make sense of evidence and data to make recommendations for future action, we hope that you will begin to see the connection between social work research and social work practice in the following case study.

 Box 9.2   Case study

A student social worker is on placement at a family contact centre. They are sitting in the corner of the family room supervising and observing the interactions between a father, Jay, who has recently been released from prison after serving a reduced 12-month sentence for aggravated assault, and his 2-year-old daughter, Holly.

At the end of the meeting, the student informs the onsite supervisor that Holly is demonstrating non-organic failure to thrive. In substantiating the concerns, the student refers to a book by Mary Sheridan. The book was published in 1997 and is titled *From Birth to Five Years: Children's Developmental Progress*.

The student explains that Mary Sheridan's book states that a 2-year-old should be able to run and climb, build a tower from six or more bricks, spoonfeed themselves and drink from a cup. The student remarks that for the entire meeting with her father, Holly did not run around, climb on the furniture or play with the building blocks that were on the floor. The student also pointed out to the onsite supervisor that when her father gave Holly a yoghurt and a cup of juice she left them untouched. Referring to attachment theory, described in the same book, the student also said that Holly had an insecure attachment because she did not cry when Jay left the centre.

As the book is based on the pioneering work of Mary Sheridan, and because it is widely regarded as the go-to reference for health, education and social care professionals, or anyone concerned with the developmental progress of pre-school children, the student is confident that their concerns about the daughter are valid.

Questions:

1. Based on the information that has been provided in the case study, do you share the student's concerns?
2. Why might the student's observations be problematic?
3. How can the student's concerns be verified?

As is now hopefully obvious, one of the biggest problems with the theories of social work, social sciences, humanities, biology and psychology lies in their unreflected application. If social work students are not careful, they can use the knowledge that they develop throughout their training to label, judge and even diagnose. Arguably, the one-sided or biased application of knowledge can have serious and detrimental effects on the people you are working to support. Indeed, if the student in the case study in Box 9.2 had written an official report, one that might have informed decision-making processes at a child protection case conference, for example, the consequence of making such generalised judgements would almost certainly lead to questions about the student's suitability for practice.

So, where does research fit in with all this? Well, research is defined by Smith (2009) as a systematic, organised and structured investigation that gathers evidence to answer a specific question, to identify new knowledge and to advance approaches to social work theory and practice. Just like social work research, social work practice requires you to respond to a referral, complaint or case review outcome, to identify the most reliable methods of data collection to gather reliable evidence, develop new knowledge and then verify whether the concerns or allegations that have been presented are true. Whether the allegation, concern, complaint or case review outcome is upheld or not, there will follow a series of carefully considered recommendations for any further intervention, which could be provided by the social worker or through universal services. It is here that the similarity between social work research and social work practice is complete.

The main concern with the student's conclusions presented in the case study speaks directly to analysis. While the intention to raise concerns about the child might have been honest and well-meaning, the apparent lack of assessment, evidence, synthesis and analysis meant that a judgemental conclusion was made. The student did not engage in a systematic, organised and structured investigation. While it is commendable that the student attempted to apply their knowledge of Sheridan's (1997) explanation of child development, they did not seek to critically analyse this knowledge against other available evidence, including that which could have been gleaned from indigenous knowledge.

The most reliable way to gather indigenous knowledge is to speak directly to the people you are working to support. We know that those people who experience social work value nothing more than the feeling that they are being listened to (Rogers et al., 2016). However, some of the people you are working to support may have encountered many different social workers and other professionals. They may be tired of telling their story and may become frustrated if you begin a conversation without any prior knowledge of them or their situation. For this reason, we strongly encourage you to apply the skills advanced in Chapter 3 to critically read a person's case file and chronology (where this is available) prior to your first visit, so that you have a good working knowledge of previous interventions. The caveat associated with this position has been advanced by the disability model, for instance, where people who are living with a physical, sensory or multiple impairment prefer you to meet them before reading any case file so that you do not make any judgements about them because of a diagnosed disability (Barnes and Mercer, 2004).

Danger point: avoiding blame

If we consider the fact that social work responds to referrals to investigate allegations or concerns pertaining to risk, harm, vulnerability or capacity, and acknowledge the possibility that people might not consent to our involvement in their private family lives, we can also consider the possibility of conflict. If a person resents, feels threatened or intimidated by or is suspicious about your involvement and intentions, it is reasonable to consider that the relationship with you may not be entirely candid. One reactive risk of working with people who might not welcome your involvement in their lives is to blame them, or use a developing knowledge of mental health, theories of grief, separation and loss (Kübler-Ross, 1969), or concepts of disguised compliance to label them and their relationship with you as resistant or worse. Indeed, the opportunity for blame becomes magnified unless the mirror of reflexivity is turned in on practice so that an accurate analytical judgement can be made (see Chapter 8).

Of course, the same point could be extended to all those people social workers work to support, but it is still important to avoid asking people to repeat information that they have already given to another professional.

Gathering indigenous knowledge directly from the people you are working to support requires a confident and competent appreciation and mastery of the knowledge, values and skills that have been presented in this book. This is the reason why this chapter's focus on analytical assessments and report writing is the last word on critical reflection. We have explained that social work is a privileged profession that can exercise significant power over others. This power and the general perception of social work is one reason why gathering honest and detailed indigenous knowledge to inform analytical assessments can be difficult.

There are several theories and concepts that assist in an understanding of relationships. The one we will focus on here is Tuckman's (1965) 'forming–storming–norming–performing' model of group development. Although the original concept is over 50 years old, it continues to provide a good introduction to group work dynamics. Developed to include two other stages, 'adjourning and transforming', it is one of the better-known team development theories and has formed the basis of many further ideas since its conception (see Box 9.3).

Tuckman's (1965) model is useful to social work for many reasons. It can help you recognise and reflect on the work that you are doing with individuals, families and communities, but it is also an important tool to help you to make sense of the group work that you complete in your professional training and career. At the outset of this chapter, we mentioned the need for you to actively engage in the composition of the multi-agency team. While there are some instances where a meeting of professionals may be convened, and the person or people you are training to support will not be invited to attend, it is critical that you include their perspective. It is equally important that you view the people you are training to support as active, influential and equal members. They might not be paid for being part of this team, but to fully investigate a situation, and to emphasise the importance of indigenous knowledge, it is essential that they are able to recognise that they are key members of the multi-agency team.

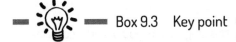 **Box 9.3   Key point**

Forming

You have been asked to complete a task with an individual, a family, community or multi-agency team. Before the meeting, you might send a letter introducing yourself, but that opportunity often depends on time and the nature of the referral. During the initial meeting, you explain the purpose of your work. On some occasions, when working with an individual, a family or community, you will also let people know about their right to complain and their right to independent legal advice or advocacy. During this stage, the people you meet will not trust you because they do not know you. It is important that you spend time explaining the systematic, organised and structured assessment that you intend to conduct and how you may use that information. The forming stage presents an important opportunity for you to build relationships, build trust and challenge initial impressions. There is no defined time for this stage of team development.

Storming

As you develop relationships and trust, you will begin to address the allocated task hopefully by applying a mixture of procedural, questioning and exchange models of assessment. Different perceptions about social work and conflict may begin to emerge if this stage of group work development is not managed carefully. If you seek to engage people in an assessment without applying reflexivity or models of pre-reflection, this phase can be very destructive. Relationships with the people you are training to support will be made or broken in this phase, and some may never recover. In extreme cases, the work that you do as a social worker will become stuck in the storming phase. It is essential that you have strong facilitative leadership skills in this phase. There is no defined time for this stage of team development.

Norming

As you move out of the storming phase you will enter the norming phase. This tends to be a move towards harmonious working practices, where you can agree on the ground rules and values that underpin your involvement and working partnerships. In the ideal situation, trusting relationships will enable people to accept your involvement and recognise the contribution that you could make. At this stage your onsite supervisor may recognise your ability to work independently and allow you to take more responsibility for the work that you do. In the same way, you may begin to trust the people you are working with and recognise them as equal partners in your intervention. As you begin to work more independently, your analysis of the situation

(Continued)

(Continued)

should become more accurate. The risk during this stage is that you become complacent about the reason for your involvement and lose sight of the reasons why you are
involved in the first place.

Performing

You may never reach the performing phase, which is essentially a period of high performance, in your social work training because your time on placement may be limited.
Performing teams are identified by high levels of independence, motivation, knowledge and competence, as usually associated with long-term teams. You may recognise
whether you are in the performing stage if you can explain how the analysis of a situation is collaborative because it is formed by the indigenous knowledge of others.

Adjourning and transforming

This is the important final phase of ending relationships with the people you are supporting. You may write a letter to the people you have been working with, outlining
the reasons why you have enjoyed working with them. Because of your involvement,
the people you have been supporting should be able to recognise the reasons why
you were involved and sometimes provide you with feedback on the things that you
did well and the things that you could improve. As the people you have been supporting will remember you for the rest of their lives, it is important that you do not
minimise the importance of saying goodbye.

Although Tuckman (1965) provides a useful introductory understanding of group
working and group dynamics, it should be noted that any relationship can return to
any phase within the model if it experiences a change, for example, a review of the reasons why social work is involved or when there is a change in team composition. While
changes to the dynamics of the working relationships that you have with individuals,
families, communities or multi-agency teams may be confusing to you, it is important,
as we shall now see, that you remain reflexive and avoid blaming or fatalistic language
in the reports that you write.

Writing skills for practice

The task of writing (whether it be a case record, an assessment or a formal report for court
proceedings) may be considered to be one of the more mundane aspects of social work
practice. Indeed, in the much-reported problem of high caseloads, there is a particular narrative which depicts social workers as being tied to their computers, rather than being out
in the community undertaking direct work with people. However, the skill of writing for

practice is incredibly important in terms of embedding and demonstrating critical reflection and analysis, for clarification, accountability and professional responsibility (Jones, 2016). Indeed, writing in social work is a professional activity and should not be considered as peripheral. You should also consider the long-term nature of the written word in that what you write about a person or family will stay on record possibly for longer than you are part of their life, on placement, or employed, with an agency. Therefore, it is important that what you write is as factually accurate as possible, that claims are verifiable in that there is evidence to support judgements and decisions, and that it is objective. Do not forget that writing is a powerful form of communication (Rogers et al., 2016).

In everyday practice, written documents serve several functions including:

- To record and transfer referral information
- To serve as a chronology (a historical record) for an individual or a family
- To further knowledge and understanding to enhance a new practitioner's work with an individual or a family
- To document data gathering, evidence and analysis
- To record judgements and decision-making
- To provide an account of actions and interventions
- To provide a register of communication (telephone calls, home visits, multi-agency meetings)
- To produce a formal report in court proceedings.

As a student in training to support people who become engaged with social work, writing will be an important aspect of your professional development in terms of evidencing your capacity for critical reflection and critical analysis, as well as the ability to apply legislation, theories and other forms of knowledge such as research or indigenous knowledge (see Chapter 4). In this final section, we offer a practical guide to case recording and report writing – the two main written products that you will be tasked with during your social work studies (when completing a professional placement) and when you move into practice as a qualified social worker.

Case recording

Case recording is constituted in a number of forms including telephone calls, case notes, emails, referral information, risk assessment, support plans, and so on. In this section, we will focus on case notes. Case notes, as opposed to formal reports, are generally never read by professionals outside your agency. As such, as with any piece of writing, you should consider the audience. With case notes, this is commonly your social work colleagues, your line manager and anyone involved in auditing files for your agency (this is undertaken to check issues such as quality and timeliness). Case notes are important as they paint a picture, over time, of an individual and/or family in relation to risk, need, vulnerability and capacity and how social work (and other) interventions have been received and helped to manage those issues. Case notes have an important element of indicating change or patterns over time by illustrating the dynamic nature of risk, need, vulnerability and capacity in terms of decline, improvement, engagement with services and communication between social work professionals and those we are working with. Poor case notes equal poor practice as there is a danger that information is not communicated properly and even lost, risk is not recorded, evidence of engagement is negated, and decision-making becomes partially informed. Good case notes require you to be organised, to be able to extract and articulate key information, and to understand the importance of transparent activity and decision-making. Review the guidance in Box 9.4 on good practice in case note recording. Then look at Box 9.5 and consider the two case notes about Jay and Holly in light of the good practice guidance.

 Box 9.4   Key point

Good practice in case recording

This list is not exhaustive, but includes some of the well-documented and agreed principles for quality case notes:

Remember the three Cs for presenting information: records should be *clear, concise* and *consistent* in the information that you present.

Records should be written from an objective stance: this means that they are factual, accurate and supported by evidence where possible. Where evidence is missing, do not speculate or make assumptions.

Timeliness is important, and you should aim to complete any case notes as soon as possible after receiving information or after an event such as a telephone call or home visit.

Records should include factual information such as date and time. Any later amendments or update should also show the date and time of these changes. This ensures transparency.

Jargon, abbreviations, acronyms, metaphors and other conversational language should be avoided at all times.

 Box 9.5   Key point

Good versus poor case notes

Case note 1: How *not* to write a case note

During contact two weeks ago on Thursday 2018 I supervised Jay and Holly. It was the first contact since he had got out of prison. I could see that the daughter was demonstrating a failure to thrive in line with the guidance in Mary Sheridan's book, *From Birth to Five Years: Children's Developmental Progress*. A 2-year-old should be able to run and climb, build a tower from six or more bricks, spoon-feed themselves and drink from a cup. During supervision she did not run around, climb on the furniture or play with the building blocks that were on the floor. Attachment theory tells us that the daughter has an insecure attachment as she did not cry when her father left. An assessment needs to be done to explore these further with action to help the daughter to thrive in her development.

Case note 2: Embedding good practice in case notes

Supervised contact session between Jay Merengue DOB: 2/2/1970 and Holly Merengue DOB: 3/7/2016. The session was held between 4 and 4.30pm on 17/9/2018. This was the first contact since Jay was released from prison on 11/8/2018. During contact some limited communication was observed between Jay and Holly, but they did not play together with the equipment or toys in the room. Holly sat on Jay's knee for a half of the session with a book. For the other half she sat on the floor near him with the same book. Just before the end of the session Jay asked if he could give Holly a drink and yoghurt (although she didn't want either). At the end of the session Holly did not get upset when she left Jay to return home (taken by another member of the team, Ian McBride).

Action: To meet with Jay prior to the next session to discuss how we can support him, as a parent, to develop a positive relationship with Holly (suggesting ideas for reading with Holly, playing, etc.).

Rochelle John, Student social worker, Family Contact Centre, 18/9/2018.

Questions:

Compare the two case notes. Can you identify good and poor practice in writing case notes? You should clearly be able to see more evidence of an objective and factual recording of the session itself in case note 2. This also contains more factual information that is needed for case records (names, times, dates, dates of birth). Observations are made without judgements, but instead these are used to propose an action. The action itself may be underpinned by knowledge about Jay and Holly (lack of prior contact and therefore an inability to form a bond due to Jay's absence) and theory (in relation to parenting and child development and what helps bonds and secure attachment to develop).

Imagine that you are Jay and that you read case note 1. How do you think you might react? Now read case note 2 as though you are Jay; would you react differently? The answer must be 'yes'. It is good practice to consider how your records might be read and interpreted by the people you are writing about.

Before we move on to think about writing formal reports, there is a point to be made about timeliness (as identified in the 'good practice in case recording' principles above), particularly as this is an important aspect of any form of written record. For some time, there has been a particular narrative that is used in writing about the social work profession and practice contexts in terms of the neoliberal model that influences how agencies are structured and managed as well as how services are delivered, monitored and appraised. This neoliberal model has resulted in market drivers such as the adoption of performance indicators and timescales. The important thing about our case records, though, is not timescales but *timeliness*. There is an important difference. You should use your professional judgement in terms of what is and what is not acceptable in the length of time between events and the timeliness of when you then record this. For example, if you, like Rochelle in case note 1 in Box 9.5, wait two weeks before writing your account of a supervised contact session, how likely is it that your record will be inaccurate in terms of what you observed? Time management is a key skill, and will rely upon you to manage your time, work tasks, visits and so on, but you will need to use judgement to decide when and how you undertake these demands.

Report writing

While on placement, it is likely that you will also have to write a formal report, whether this is following an assessment or a review, for a child protection conference, mental health review or court proceedings. In accordance with the principles for case recording, your report should be accurate, factual, timely and objective. You should reflect on the purpose and audience in the process of considering what must be included and in what context. For example, writing a report to request resources (a short break for foster carers where the audience is a resources panel) or a court report (where the audience is a judge, among others) might require a different emphasis or different uses of evidence. In either case, professional judgements, decision-making and planning should all be based on evidence. Bogg (2012: 3) proffers some sound principles for effective report writing:

1. The purpose of the report is explicit.
2. All information and decision-making are based on evidence and that evidence is clearly articulated.
3. All sources of information are clearly reported.
4. Any opinions or third-party reports are identified.
5. Appropriate language and tone are used throughout.
6. The report is an appropriate length and the writing is concise.
7. The report is signed and dated by the author.

These principles form the foundation for a professionally produced report which is evidenced, transparent and fit for purpose. The structure and format may differ depending on the task, the field of social work (children, mental health, or adults), the audience (a social work manager, multi-agency forum or court) and in terms of agency culture and protocols. Whatever the context, the principles should be employed, as should the commitment to timeliness. The style and tone of written language are also important as reports are generally prescriptive (that is, they are written with a specific focus). Reports should be clear and concise, but with necessary detail and evidence. In previous years, social workers have been criticised publicly for employing 'opaque' language (Lishman, 2009). Remember that the points that you are making need to be explicit and not hidden by flowery or abstract language. You may find yourself reusing the same word, in which case you could use a thesaurus to find a synonym. However, care is needed as the meaning can be obscured in this way. We accept that, as a student in training, you may never have written a formal report prior to your studies. It may be useful to consider the GAS model (Figure 9.1) which can help you remember the key principles of effective professional report writing. Then try the activity in Box 9.6.

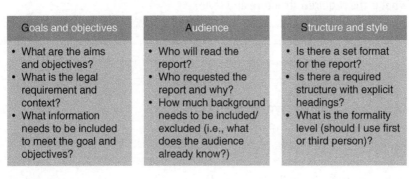

Figure 9.1 GAS model

Source: adapted from Bogg (2012)

 Box 9.6   Activity

Applying GAS principles

Reconsider the current situation with Jay and Holly. After a conversation with Jay he admits that he feels out of touch with his role and status as the father of a young child as all his other children are grown up. He has not engaged in consistent contact with Holly nor been able to develop a relationship with her as Jay and Holly's mother separated when she was pregnant. Jay went to prison soon after Holly was born. Jay is determined to stay out of prison and wishes to be a good father. Jay accepted the offer of a referral for him to attend a parenting course. The only one you can find is due to start soon and it is offered by another department at your local authority. You have to make a case for Jay to have a funded place. This report will be considered by the resources panel. Think about the report that you would write.

(Continued)

(Continued)

- What are the goals and objectives?

....

....

....

....

- Who is the audience?

....

....

....

....

- What is the required structure and style?

....

....

....

....

See Appendix 2 (p. 187) for some thoughts.

Integrating analysis in written records

This final section is an important one. As with academic writing (see Chapter 4), it is important to embed analysis in written records. While you may begin writing a report or assessment by thinking about all the descriptive and contextual information that needs to be provided to the reader in order for them to have a clear picture of what is happening, you also need to provide analysis and synthesise information to then underpin the judgements or proposed interventions that you include. You should embed the principles and tips in Chapter 4 on academic writing as these will also be helpful in terms of report-writing skills. In particular, consider: organisation; sequencing; critical analysis; strong transitions; the passive voice and other academic conventions (for example, objectivity versus subjectivity). Box 9.7 contains some additional pointers in terms of integrating analysis and moving beyond the tendency to describe a person or situation and describe your potential actions.

By developing analytical record-keeping and report-writing skills, you will be able to evidence professional judgements and decision-making using verifiable claims. Do not forget that your reasoned judgements will be supported by your gathered evidence, as well as indigenous knowledge, research knowledge and theory. Where there are gaps in your gathered information, do not try to plug the absence but note the gap and be explicit about actions that will be needed to address this. This adds credibility to your assessment as it indicates that you have analysed the information to establish that gaps exist. When providing detail about proposed actions and interventions, remember to take an approach to 'what works' as this will be supported by an evidence base.

 **Box 9.7   Key point**

Principles for embedding analysis in written records and reports (adapted from Rogers et al., 2016)

Good practice principles

- Identify the significance of the information that you are presenting by highlighting outcomes or the likelihood of an outcome if there is to be an intervention (or no intervention and therefore no change).
- When describing outcomes, use connectives (such as 'as a result', 'because', 'since' and 'therefore') to indicate cause and effect.
- Assess the credibility of evidence and provide an appraisal of its value or limitations.
- Weigh up one piece of evidence against another.
- Ensure that fact and opinion are differentiated and credit these different sources of information.
- Use connectives (such as 'whereas', 'though', 'unless', 'on the other hand') to illustrate contrast and comparison.

SUMMARY

This final chapter has discussed the centrality of analysis in the process of assessment, which involves several skills that are covered elsewhere in this book. These include: critical knowledge; critical writing; professional judgement and decision-making; critical analysis; and critical reflection. We have highlighted the importance of evidence-based and evidence-informed practice drawing on the indigenous knowledge of the people that social work seeks to support. In our use of Tuckman's model of group development as a case study, we have highlighted some barriers and enablers in working with people in the assessment process. Finally, this chapter builds on Chapter 4, which introduced critical writing as a fundamental skill, to consider integrating analysis into the written records that we will be tasked with producing in the workplace.

Having read this chapter, you should be able to:

- Understand the importance of indigenous knowledge
- Understand the importance of analysis in the process of social work assessment and in how this translates to the written records that we are required to produce in our everyday work
- Articulate Tuckman's model of group development
- Recognise the importance of valid substantiation when constructing arguments
- Write critically and with confidence.

FURTHER READING

Bogg, D. (2012). *Report Writing*. Maidenhead: Open University Press.

Dyke, C. (2016). *Writing Analytical Assessments in Social Work*. St Albans: Critical Publishing.

CONCLUSION

This book has provided you with theoretical, conceptual and practical information intended to guide you in the application of the critical and analytical skills required for studies in social work education and social work practice. In Part I we began by exploring critical thinking in a conceptual chapter, with some practical activities, to help you to understand the foundational understanding of critical skills. In Part II we offered both theoretical reading and practical tips highlighting the key skills needed when you begin your studies as a social work student. This part opened with an exploration of critical knowledge. This theme underpins the remaining chapters which centred on skill-building in the areas of critical reading, critical writing and critical reflection. The mix of theoretical and practical content in each chapter was intended as a way to help you understand the importance of these skills, but also as a means to develop your abilities in each.

The book is written for anyone studying pre-qualifying social work, for someone who may have been introduced to the topics in previous studies, but also for someone who has not studied for some time or who studied a discipline that is unrelated to the social sciences. This reflects the diversity of the social work student body more generally. In Part III we build on the themes so far and turn your attention to how these are required in social work practice. We explore critical thinking in the realms of making professional judgements, decision-making, completing analytical assessments and the administrative processes that record each of these (in case recording). Recognising that these skills are required in both the academic and work environment, we have included real-world case studies and activities to enable you to consider the value of and to practise critical and analytical skills with lots of opportunities to apply these to encourage the application, rather than merely the conceptual understanding of what is meant by 'critical thinking'.

While social work is a changeable field and discipline, we have pointed to some of the contemporary contexts (such as neoliberalism) that provide everyday challenges in practice. However, some of the challenges for students are more fundamental than that. We wrote this book using our experiential knowledge as social work lecturers, having worked with many students who struggle to embed critical thinking and analysis from the start, and who begin their studies not really knowing what is meant when we talk of being 'critical'. This is why we begin the book by paying attention to the very notion of being critical and we underline this with the awareness and central importance of using knowledge, in its various forms, with a critical eye – being able to question sources of knowledge and being tentative about using evidence in the processes of judgement and decision-making. We encourage you, the reader, to develop and embed analytical skills in all aspects of your practice and to strive to be the best social worker you can possibly be.

GLOSSARY

Analysis: a detailed examination of the elements or structure of something.

Anti-oppressive practice: an important model for identifying and maintaining empowering client relationships in the context of existing oppression in society and practice.

Assessment: involves gathering and assessing information about a situation using appropriate social work knowledge and theory to develop a plan that involves all the relevant parties.

Capacity: refers to something you can do, or the amount of a certain task that you are able to do.

Concept: an abstract idea.

Confirmation bias: the tendency to search for, interpret, favour, and recall information in a way that confirms one's pre-existing beliefs or stereotypical judgements.

Critical analysis: a detailed analysis and assessment of something, especially a literary, philosophical or political theory.

Critical reflection: a reasoning process systematically used to make meaning of an experience.

Critical thinking: the objective analysis and evaluation of an issue in order to form a judgement.

Cultural relativism: the principle of regarding the beliefs, values and practices of a culture from the viewpoint of that culture itself.

Disguised compliance: giving the appearance of co-operation in order to avoid raising suspicions, to dilute concerns and ultimately to reduce or negate professional intervention.

Ecological systems theory: identifies five environmental systems with which an individual interacts. These include the individual's relationships within families, communities and the wider society.

Empirical evidence: the information received by means of the senses, particularly by observation and documentation of patterns through experimentation or research.

Empiricism: the theory that all knowledge is based on experience derived from the senses.

Epistemology: the theory of knowledge especially with regard to its methods, validity and scope, and the distinction between justifiable belief and opinion.

Evidence-based practice: a process which involves critical thinking and evaluation of information to determine the most effective method of intervention.

Evidence-informed practice: used to design social work methods of practice and activities using information about what works.

Expert by experience: the view that the people you are training to support are experts in their own situations.

Grey literature: unpublished research papers, including government reports, PhD theses and some monographs.

Human rights: these are not privileges to be earned or gifts that governments can give or take away at will, but part of what it means to be human.

Indigenous knowledge: the knowledge of the expert by experience.

Knowledge: facts, information and skills acquired through experience or education; the theoretical or practical understanding of a subject.

Law: the system of rules which a country or community recognises as regulating the actions of its members and which it may enforce by the imposition of penalties.

Learning outcomes: statements that describe the knowledge or skills students should acquire by the end of an assignment, class or course.

Mixed methods research: involves qualitative and quantitative projects being mixed in more than one stage of the study.

Objectivity: the state or quality of being objective. In social work, objectivity is achieved when practice lacks bias and is driven by verifiable facts, not by personal beliefs or feelings.

Ontology: the philosophical study of the nature of being, becoming, existence or reality.

Paradigm: a world view that underpins the theory of a subject, or a typical example or model.

Policy: a system of principles or guidelines that guide decisions or behaviour.

Positive risk-taking: the notion that measuring risk involves balancing the positive benefits gained from taking risks against the negative effects of attempting to avoid risk in its entirety.

Practice wisdom: encompasses both the art (creativity, adaptability, tacit knowledge) and the science (use of theory, research and evidence bases) of social work.

Praxis: the practical side and practice of a profession and field of study.

Qualitative research: an approach to researching the social world which focuses on language and subjective experiences. Qualitative research seeks to interpret meanings and provide insights into social life.

Quantitative research: an approach which emphasises the importance of numerical and quantifiable data in the collection and analysis of data. As a research strategy, it incorporates a natural science model and is concerned with objectivity and fact.

Reflection in action: the ability to reflect on and analyse a situation and your practice at the time.

Reflection on action: the ability to reflect on and analyse a situation and your practice after the event.

Reflexivity: there are many definitions of reflexivity. In its basic form, it refers to the capacity to recognise your impact on an individual, and their effects on you (cause and effect). It requires an analysis of personal, social and intersubjective processes.

Resilience: the capacity to recover from risk or adversity.

Risk: a situation or phenomenon which exposes someone to danger, loss or harm.

Rule of optimism: the tendency to interpret data in a rather hopeful and positive way, as a willingness to be compliant is confused with an actual willingness to accept the need to change. A process of rationalisation is undertaken which minimises risk.

Skill: expertise and the ability to do something well.

Social constructivism: a sociological theory which proffers that knowledge is created in social processes through interaction with others.

Strengths-based approach: a model for social work which seeks to emphasise an individual's strengths and successes, rather than their failures and transgressions.

Structural inequality: a sociological concept that views marginal groups of people in society as experiencing an unequal status and disparity of experiences due to particular structures (for example, the law, or societal norms).

Subjectivity: the quality or position of being based on or influenced by personal feelings, tastes, opinions or experiences.

Synthesis: the combination of a number of elements to form a whole.

Systematic review: a literature review which employs a transparent, systematic methodology which can easily be replicated.

Tacit knowledge: knowledge that is known implicitly, rather than explicitly. It has also been termed 'knowing in practice' (Schön, 1983) and 'unconscious knowing' (Osmond, 2005). An example of this is the ability to speak a language or drive a car.

Theory/theoretical knowledge: a set of ideas or principles that are intended to explain a particular thing.

User and carer knowledge: a type of knowledge that people have about themselves or their world. Another way of thinking about people in this way is to consider them to be *experts by experience*.

Values: the beliefs or attitudes that are held by an individual or shared by a community that hold some notion of what is good or bad about a particular thing.

APPENDIX 1

Learning Styles Questionnaire

This questionnaire is designed to find out your preferred learning style(s). Over the years you have probably developed learning 'habits' that help you benefit more from some experiences than from others. Since you are probably unaware of this, this questionnaire will help you pinpoint your learning preferences so that you are in a better position to select learning experiences that suit your style and have a greater understanding of those that suit the style of others.

This is an internationally proven tool designed by Peter Honey and Alan Mumford.

There is no time limit to this questionnaire. It will probably take you 10–15 minutes. The accuracy of the results depends on how honest you can be. There are no right or wrong answers.

If you agree more than you disagree with a statement, put a tick by it.

If you disagree more than you agree, put a cross by it.

Be sure to mark each item with either a tick or a cross.

1	I have strong beliefs about what is right and wrong, good and bad	☐
2	I often act without considering the possible consequences	☐
3	I tend to solve problems using a step-by-step approach	☐
4	I believe that formal procedures and policies restrict people	☐
5	I have a reputation for saying what I think, simply and directly	☐
6	I often find that actions based on feelings are as sound as those based on careful thought and analysis	☐
7	I like the sort of work where I have time for thorough preparation and implementation	☐
8	I regularly question people about their basic assumptions	☐
9	What matters most is whether something works in practice	☐
10	I actively seek out new experiences	☐

11   When I hear about a new idea or approach I immediately start working out how to apply it in practice ☐

12   I am keen on self-discipline such as watching my diet, taking regular exercise, sticking to a fixed routine, etc. ☐

13   I take pride in doing a thorough job ☐

14   I get on best with logical, analytical people and less well with spontaneous, 'irrational' people ☐

15   I take care over the interpretation of data available to me and avoid jumping to conclusions ☐

16   I like to reach a decision carefully after weighing up many alternatives ☐

17   I'm attracted more to novel, unusual ideas than to practical ones ☐

18   I don't like disorganised things and prefer to fit things into a coherent pattern ☐

19   I accept and stick to laid down procedures and policies so long as I regard them as an efficient way of getting the job done ☐

20   I like to relate my actions to a general principle ☐

21   In discussions I like to get straight to the point ☐

22   I tend to have distant, rather formal relationships with people at work ☐

23   I thrive on the challenge of tackling something new and different ☐

24   I enjoy fun-loving, spontaneous people ☐

25   I pay meticulous attention to detail before coming to a conclusion ☐

26   I find it difficult to produce ideas on impulse ☐

27   I believe in coming to the point immediately ☐

28   I am careful not to jump to conclusions too quickly ☐

29   I prefer to have as many resources of information as possible – the more data to think over the better ☐

30   Flippant people who don't take things seriously enough usually irritate me ☐

31   I listen to other people's points of view before putting my own forward ☐

32   I tend to be open about how I'm feeling ☐

33   In discussions I enjoy watching the manoeuvrings of the other participants ☐

34   I prefer to respond to events on a spontaneous, flexible basis rather than plan things out in advance ☐

35   I tend to be attracted to techniques such as network analysis, flow charts, branching programs, contingency planning, etc. ☐

36   It worries me if I have to rush out a piece of work to meet a tight deadline ☐

37   I tend to judge people's ideas on their practical merits ☐

38 Quiet, thoughtful people tend to make me feel uneasy ☐

39 I often get irritated by people who want to rush things ☐

40 It is more important to enjoy the present moment than to think about the past or future ☐

41 I think that decisions based on a thorough analysis of all the information are sounder than those based on intuition ☐

42 I tend to be a perfectionist ☐

43 In discussions I usually produce lots of spontaneous ideas ☐

44 In meetings I put forward practical realistic ideas ☐

45 More often than not, rules are there to be broken ☐

46 I prefer to stand back from a situation ☐

47 I can often see inconsistencies and weaknesses in other people's arguments ☐

48 On balance I talk more than I listen ☐

49 I can often see better, more practical ways to get things done ☐

50 I think written reports should be short and to the point ☐

51 I believe that rational, logical thinking should win the day ☐

52 I tend to discuss specific things with people rather than engaging in social discussion ☐

53 I like people who approach things realistically rather than theoretically ☐

54 In discussions I get impatient with irrelevancies and digressions ☐

55 If I have a report to write I tend to produce lots of drafts before settling on the final version ☐

56 1 am keen to try things out to see if they work in practice ☐

57 I am keen to reach answers via a logical approach ☐

58 I enjoy being the one that talks a lot ☐

59 In discussions I often find I am the realist, keeping people to the point and avoiding wild speculations ☐

60 I like to ponder many alternatives before making up my mind ☐

61 In discussions with people I often find I am the most dispassionate and objective ☐

62 In discussions I'm more likely to adopt a 'low profile' than to take the lead and do most of the talking ☐

63 I like to be able to relate current actions to a longer term bigger picture ☐

64 When things go wrong I am happy to shrug it off and 'put it down to experience' ☐

65 I tend to reject wild, spontaneous ideas as being impractical ☐

66 It's best to think carefully before taking action ☐

67 On balance I do the listening rather than the talking ☐

68 I tend to be tough on people who find it difficult to adopt a logical approach ☐

69 Most times I believe the end justifies the means ☐

70 I don't mind hurting people's feelings so long as the job gets done ☐

71 I find the formality of having specific objectives and plans stifling ☐

72 I'm usually one of the people who puts life into a party ☐

73 I do whatever is expedient to get the job done ☐

74 I quickly get bored with methodical, detailed work ☐

75 I am keen on exploring the basic assumptions, principles and theories underpinning things and events ☐

76 I'm always interested to find out what people think ☐

77 I like meetings to be run on methodical lines, sticking to a laid down agenda, etc. ☐

78 I steer clear of subjective or ambiguous topics ☐

79 I enjoy the drama and excitement of a crisis situation ☐

80 People often find me insensitive to their feelings ☐

Scoring and Interpreting the Learning Styles Questionnaire

The Questionnaire is scored by awarding one point for each ticked item. There are no points for crossed items. Simply indicate on the lists below which items were ticked by circling the appropriate question number.

2	7	1	5
4	13	3	9
6	15	8	11
10	16	12	19
17	25	14	21
23	28	18	27
24	29	20	35
32	31	22	37
34	33	26	44
38	36	30	49
40	39	42	50
43	41	47	53
45	46	51	54

48	52	57	56
58	55	61	59
64	60	63	65
71	62	68	69
72	66	75	70
74	67	77	73
79	76	78	80
____	____	____	____
TOTALS **Activist**	**Reflector**	**Theorist**	**Pragmatist**

Learning Styles Questionnaire Profile Based on General Norms for 1302 People

Activist	Reflector	Theorist	Pragmatist	
20	20	20	20	Very strong preference
19				
18		19	19	
17				
16		18		
15		17	18	
14				
13	18	16	17	
12	17	15	16	Strong preference
	16			
11	15	14	15	
10	14	13	14	Moderate
9	13	12	13	
8				
7	12	11	12	

(Continued)

(Continued)

Activist	Reflector	Theorist	Pragmatist	
6	11	10	11	Low preference
5	10	9	10	
4	9	8	9	
3	8	7	8	Very low preference
	7	6	7	
	6	5	6	
2	5	4	4	
	4	3	3	
	3			
1	2	2	2	
	1	1	1	
0	0	0	0	

Learning Styles – General Descriptions

Activists

Activists involve themselves fully and without bias in new experiences. They enjoy the here and now and are happy to be dominated by immediate experiences. They are open-minded, not sceptical, and this tends to make them enthusiastic about anything new. Their philosophy is: 'I'll try anything once'. They tend to act first and consider the consequences afterwards. Their days are filled with activity. They tackle problems by brainstorming. As soon as the excitement from one activity has died down, they are busy looking for the next. They tend to thrive on the challenge of new experiences but are bored with implementation and longer-term consolidation. They are gregarious people constantly involving themselves with others but, in doing so, they seek to centre all activities on themselves.

Reflectors

Reflectors like to stand back to ponder experiences and observe them from many different perspectives. They collect data, both first hand and from others, and prefer to think about it thoroughly before coming to any conclusion. The thorough collection and analysis of data about experiences and events is what counts so they tend to postpone reaching definitive conclusions for as long as possible. Their philosophy is to be cautious. They are thoughtful people who like to consider all possible angles and implications before making a move. They prefer to take a back seat in meetings and discussions. They enjoy observing other people in action. They listen to others and get the drift of the discussion before making their own points. They tend to adopt a low profile and have a slightly distant, tolerant unruffled air about them. When they act, it is part of a wide picture which includes the past as well as the present and others' observations as well as their own.

Theorists

Theorists adapt and integrate observations into complex but logically sound theories. They think problems through in a vertical, step-by-step logical way. They assimilate disparate facts into coherent theories. They tend to be perfectionists who won't rest easy until things are tidy and fit into a rational scheme. They like to analyse and synthesise. They are keen on basic assumptions, principles, theories, models and systems thinking. Their philosophy prizes rationality and logic. 'If it's logical it's good'. Questions they frequently ask are: 'Does it make sense?' 'How does this fit with that?' 'What are the basic assumptions?' They tend to be detached, analytical and dedicated to rational objectivity rather than anything subjective or ambiguous. Their approach to problems is consistently logical. This is their 'mental set' and they rigidly reject anything that doesn't fit with it. They prefer to maximise certainty and feel uncomfortable with subjective judgements, lateral thinking and anything flippant.

Pragmatists

Pragmatists are keen on trying out ideas, theories and techniques to see if they work in practice. They positively search out new ideas and take the first opportunity to experiment with applications. They are the sorts of people who return from management courses brimming with new ideas that they want to try out in practice. They like to get on with things and act quickly and confidently on ideas that attract them. They tend to be impatient with ruminating and open-ended discussions. They are essentially practical, down to earth people who like making practical decisions and solving problems. They respond to problems and opportunities 'as a challenge'. Their philosophy is: 'There is always a better way' and 'if it works it's good'.

In descending order of likelihood, the most common combinations are:

1st Reflector/Theorist

2nd Theorist/Pragmatist

3rd Reflector/Pragmatist

4th Activist/Pragmatist

Learning styles - a further perspective

Activists

Activists learn best from activities where:

- There are new experiences/problems/opportunities from which to learn.
- They can engross themselves in short 'here and now' activities such as business games, competitive teamwork tasks, role-playing exercises.
- There is excitement/drama/crisis and things chop and change with a range of diverse activities to tackle.
- They have a lot of the limelight/high visibility, i.e. they can 'chair' meetings, lead discussions and give presentations.
- They are allowed to generate ideas without constraints of policy or structure or feasibility.
- They are thrown in at the deep end with a task they think is difficult, i.e. when set a challenge with inadequate resources and adverse conditions.
- They are involved with other people, i.e. bouncing ideas off them, solving problems as part of a team.
- It is appropriate to 'have a go'.

Activists learn least from, and may react against, activities where:

- Learning involves a passive role, i.e. listening to lectures, monologues, explanations, statements of how things should be done, reading, watching.
- They are asked to stand back and not be involved.
- They are required to assimilate, analyse and interpret lots of 'messy' data.
- They are required to engage in solitary work, i.e. reading, writing, thinking on their own.
- They are asked to assess beforehand what they will learn, and to appraise afterwards what they have learned.
- They are offered statements they see as 'theoretical', i.e. an explanation of cause or background.
- They are asked to repeat essentially the same activity over and over again, i.e. when practising.
- They have precise instructions to follow with little room for manoeuvre.
- They are asked to do a thorough job, i.e. attend to detail, tie up loose ends, dot the i's, cross the t's.

Summary of strengths

- Flexible and open minded.
- Happy to have a go.
- Happy to be exposed to new situations.
- Optimistic about anything new and therefore unlikely to resist change.

Summary of weaknesses

- Tendency to take the immediately obvious action without thinking.
- Often take unnecessary risks.
- Tendency to do too much themselves and hog the limelight.

- Rush into action without sufficient preparation.
- Get bored with implementation/consolidation.

Key questions for activists

- Shall I learn something new, i.e. that I didn't know/couldn't do before?
- Will there be a wide variety of different activities? (I don't want to sit and listen for more than an hour at a stretch!)
- Will it be OK to have a go/let my hair down/make mistakes/have fun?
- Shall I encounter some tough problems and challenges?
- Will there be other like-minded people to mix with?

Reflectors

Reflectors learn best from activities where:

- They are allowed or encouraged to watch/think/chew over activities.
- They are able to stand back from events and listen/observe, i.e. observing a group at work, taking a back seat in a meeting, watching a film or video.
- They are allowed to think before acting, to assimilate before commencing, i.e. time to prepare, a chance to read in advance a brief giving background data.
- They can carry out some painstaking research, i.e. investigate, assemble information and probe to get to the bottom of things.
- They have the opportunity to review what has happened, what they have learned.
- They are asked to produce carefully considered analyses and reports.
- They are helped to exchange views with other people without danger, i.e. by prior agreement, within a structured learning experience.
- They can reach a decision in their own time without pressure and tight deadlines.

Reflectors learn least from, and may react against, activities where:

- They are 'forced' into the limelight, i.e. to act as leader/chairman, to role-play in front of on-lookers.
- They are involved in situations which require action without planning.
- They are pitched into doing something without warning, i.e. to produce an instant reaction, to produce an off-the-top-of-the-head idea.
- They are given insufficient data on which to base a conclusion.
- They are given cut and dried instructions of how things should be done.
- They are worried by time pressures or rushed from one activity to another.
- In the interests of expediency, they have to make short cuts or do a superficial job.

Summary of strengths

- Careful.
- Thorough and methodical.

- Thoughtful.
- Good at listening to others and assimilating information.
- Rarely jump to conclusions.

Summary of weaknesses

- Tendency to hold back from direct participation.
- Slow to make up their minds and reach a decision.
- Tendency to be too cautious and not take enough risks.
- Not assertive - they aren't particularly forthcoming and have no 'small talk'.

Key questions for reflectors

- Shall I be given adequate time to consider, assimilate and prepare?
- Will there be opportunities/facilities to assemble the relevant information?
- Will there be opportunities to listen to other people's points of view - preferably a wide cross-section of people with a variety of views?
- Shall I be under pressure to be slapdash or to extemporise?

Theorists

Theorists learn best from activities where:

- What is being offered is part of a system, model, concept, theory.
- They have time to explore methodically the associations and inter-relationships between ideas, events and situations.
- They have the chance to question and probe the basic methodology, assumptions or logic behind something, i.e. by taking part in a question and answer session, by checking a paper for inconsistencies.
- They are intellectually stretched, i.e. by analysing a complex situation, being tested in a tutorial session, by teaching high-calibre people who ask searching questions.
- They are in structured situations with a clear purpose.
- They can listen to or read about ideas and concepts that emphasise rationality or logic and are well argued/elegant/watertight.
- They can analyse and then generalise the reasons for success or failure.
- They are offered interesting ideas and concepts even though they are not immediately relevant.
- They are required to understand and participate in complex situations.

Theorists learn least from, *and* may react against, activities where:

- They are pitch-forked into doing something without a context or an apparent purpose.
- They have to participate in situations emphasising emotions and feelings.
- They are involved in unstructured activities where ambiguity and uncertainty are high, i.e. with openended problems, on sensitivity training.
- They are asked to act or decide without a basis in policy, principle or concept.

- They are faced with a hotchpotch of alternative/contradictory techniques/methods without exploring any in depth, i.e. as on a 'once over lightly' course.
- They find the subject matter platitudinous, shallow or gimmicky.
- They feel themselves out of tune with other participants, i.e. when with lots of activists or people of lower intellectual calibre.

Summary of strengths

- Logical 'vertical' thinkers.
- Rational and objective.
- Good at asking probing questions.
- Disciplined approach.

Summary of weaknesses

- Restricted in lateral thinking.
- Low tolerance for uncertainty, disorder and ambiguity.
- Intolerant of anything subjective or intuitive.
- Full of 'shoulds, oughts and musts'.

Key questions for theorists

- Will there be lots of opportunities to question?
- Do the objectives and programme of events indicate a clear structure and purpose?
- Shall I encounter complex ideas and concepts that are likely to stretch me?
- Are the approaches to be used and concepts to be explored 'respectable', i.e. sound and valid?
- Shall I be with people of a similar calibre to myself?

Pragmatist

Pragmatists learn best from activities where:

- There is an obvious link between the subject matter and a problem or an opportunity on the job.
- They are shown techniques for doing things with obvious practical advantages, i.e. how to save time, how to make a good first impression, how to deal with awkward people.
- They have the chance to try out and practise techniques with coaching/feedback from a credible expert, i.e. someone who is successful and can do the techniques themselves.
- They are exposed to a model they can emulate, i.e. a respected boss, a demonstration from someone with a proven track record, lots of examples/anecdotes, and a film showing how it's done.
- They are given techniques currently applicable to their own job.
- They are given immediate opportunities to implement what they have learned.
- There is a high face validity in the learning activity, i.e. a good simulation, 'real' problems.
- They can concentrate on practical issues, i.e. drawing up action plans with an obvious end product, suggesting short cuts, giving tips.

Pragmatists learn least from, and may react against, activities where:

- The learning is not related to an immediate need they recognise/they cannot see, an immediate relevance/practical benefit.
- Organisers of the learning, or the event itself, seem distant from reality, i.e. 'ivory towered', all theory and general principles, pure 'chalk and talk'.
- There is no practice or clear guidelines on how to do it.
- They feel that people are going round in circles and not getting anywhere fast enough.
- There are political, managerial or personal obstacles to implementation.
- There is no apparent reward from the learning activity, i.e. more sales, shorter meetings, higher bonus, promotion.

Summary of strengths

- Keen to test things out in practice.
- Practical, down to earth, realistic.
- Businesslike – gets straight to the point.
- Technique oriented.

Summary of weaknesses

- Tendency to reject anything without an obvious application.
- Not very interested in theory or basic principles.
- Tendency to seize on the first expedient solution to a problem.
- Impatient with waffle.
- On balance, task oriented not people oriented.

Key questions for pragmatists

- Will there be ample opportunities to practise and experiment?
- Will there be lots of practical tips and techniques?
- Shall we be addressing real problems and will it result in action plans to tackle some of my current problems?
- Shall we be exposed to experts who know how to/can do it themselves?

APPENDIX 2

Chapter 3

Our analysis of Box 3.7

Sentence 1 – immediately it is clear that this is a professional view; the opinion of the 'expert by experience' is missing but may be included later (it is not).

Sentence 2 – 'well known' by whom? 'Affects everybody' – where is the evidence for this as the statistics that are then cited in sentence 3 only refer to women and children?

Sentence 3 – what is the source of this statistical information?

Sentence 4 – there is no logical evidence for this claim in terms of information that is presented in the whole summary.

Sentence 5 – this sentence contradicts earlier claims in sentence 2. Additionally, does the 1 in 4 statistic contained in sentence 2 indicate that 'most women' will experience domestic abuse? No, so the statistics are not correctly interpreted and a claim is made without any evidence.

Sentence 6 – again, this claim is faulty as it is not supported by logical and well-interpreted data.

Sentence 7 – there is no logical link between the two clauses in this sentence. That is, how does the claim that domestic abuse is a major concern for social work connect to the idea that social work is informed by one particular model (a strengths-based approach)?

Sentence 8 – great! A definition for the model.

Sentence 9 – this suggests that the researcher made an inference that social work practice for this group of practitioners was underpinned by this particular model. The sentence does not clearly draw back to domestic abuse but merely states that the discussion was about 'everyday contexts'.

Sentence 10 – can one focus group discussion verify that a strengths-based model for practice with families affected by domestic abuse is the 'gold standard' for practice? Is this claim valid, trustworthy and generalisable? No, not if based on one group discussion.

Chapter 4

Answer to Box 4.2

Process words: discuss, apply

Content words: capacity, Mental Capacity Act 2005, ethical challenges, theories of power and control

Suggested answer to Box 4.5

Draft essay plan

Title: Critically discuss the current structure of the child protection conference.

Introduction: State what will be discussed in the main body and why. This should indicate the order of the topics included in the main body discussion, which should be logical and illustrate interconnections between each topic. We suggest the first theme to get you started.

Main body:

Theme 1: Law and policy background – this integrates a critical discussion of the definition, function and remit of a child protection conference to demonstrate an understanding of the legal and policy requirement for this process.

Theme 2: Role of the conference chair (to enable the reader to understand the statutory management and governance of the child protection conference).

Theme 3: Social worker role (to provide an understanding of the process that leads to a child protection conference and the statutory role of the social worker).

Theme 4: Multi-agency partners (to critically discuss other professional members of the conference, their role and remit in relation to the social worker, the conference and what happens next).

Theme 5: Child, family and carer perspectives (you have set the scene, critically discussed the main professionals, and you should end with a powerful and critical evaluation of the inclusion of the child, family and carers).

Conclusion: This should provide a summary of the main points and argument. It should not introduce any new points for discussion.

Chapter 9

Some thoughts on Box 9.6

Goals and objectives

- To request and secure a funded place for Jay on a parenting programme
- To help Jay develop an understanding of child development and the needs of children at different ages and stages
- To help Jay develop fathering skills, such as engaging and playing with his child, with an understanding of the importance of these in helping Holly's healthy development

Audience

- Your line manager
- The resources panel
- The parenting programme manager/coordinator

Structure and style

- It is likely that the agency has a template or a set structure
- The report proforma is likely to include: background information; need assessment (with evidence); request and justification for resources; cost implications

REFERENCES

Abbas, A., Ali, M., Shahid Khan, M. and Khan, S. (2016) Personalized healthcare cloud services for disease risk assessment and wellness management using social media. *Pervasive and Mobile Computing, 28*, 81–99.

Akintayo, T., Hämäläinen, J. and Rissanen, S. (2016) Global standards and the realities of multiculturalism in social work curricula. *International Social Work, 61*(3), 395–409.

Allen, D. (2018) Roma people: Are discriminatory attitudes natural? In K. Bhatti-Sinclair and C. Smethurst (eds), *Diversity, Difference and Dilemmas: Analysing Concepts and Developing Skills* (pp. 77–94). London: Open University Press.

Allen, D. and Riding, R. (2018) *The Fragility of Professional Competence: A Preliminary Account of Child Protection Practice with Romani and Traveller Children*. Budapest: European Roma Rights Group.

Anderson, L. W. and Krathwohl, D. R. (eds) (2001) *A Taxonomy for Learning, Teaching, and Assessing: A Revision of Bloom's Taxonomy of Educational Objectives*. Boston, MA: Allyn & Bacon.

Barnes, C. and Mercer, G. (2004) *Implementing the Social Model of Disability: Theory and Research*. Leeds: Disability Press.

Beresford, P. (2000) Service users' knowledge and social work theory: Conflict or corroboration? *British Journal of Social Work, 30*(4), 489–503.

Beresford, P., Croft, S. and Adshead, L. (2008) 'We don't see her as a social worker': A service user case study of the importance of the social worker's relationship and humanity. *British Journal of Social Work, 38*, 1388–1407.

Bloom, B. S. (ed.), Engelhart, M. D., Furst, E. J., Hill, W. H. and Krathwohl, D. R. (1956) *Taxonomy of Educational Objectives, Handbook I: The Cognitive Domain*. New York: David McKay.

Bogg, D. (2012) *Report Writing*. Maidenhead: Open University Press.

Bourdieu, P. (1977) *Outline of a Theory of Practice* (Richard Nice, trans.). Cambridge: Cambridge University Press.

Bronfenbrenner, U. (1979) *The Ecology of Human Development: Experiments by Nature and Design*. Cambridge, MA: Harvard University Press.

Brookfield, S. (1995) *Becoming a Critically Reflective Teacher*. San-Francisco: Jossey-Bass.

Brown, C. (2017) *Critical Social Theory*. London: Sage.

Bryman, A. (2015) *Social Reseach Methods* (5th edn). Oxford: Oxford University Press.

CAADA (2014) *In Plain Sight: Effective Help for Children Exposed to Domestic Abuse*. Bristol: CAADA.

Carey, M. and Foster, V. (2011) Introducing 'deviant' social work: Contextualising the limits of radical social work whilst understanding (fragmented) resistance within the social work labour process. *British Journal of Social Work, 41*(3), 576–593.

Collingwood, P. (2005) Integrating theory and practice: The Three-Stage Theory Framework. *Journal of Practice Teaching, 6*(1), 6–23.

Collingwood, P., Emond, R. and Woodward, R. (2008) The theory circle: A tool for learning and for practice. *Social Work Education, 27*(1), 70–83.

Cottrell, S. (2011) *Critical Thinking Skills: Developing Effective Analysis and Argument* (2nd edn). London: Palgrave Macmillan.

Creme, P. and Lea, M. R. (1997) *Writing at University*. Buckingham: Open University Press.

Currer, C. (1986) Health concepts and illness behaviour: The case of some Pathan mothers in Britain. PhD thesis, University of Warwick.

Dalzell, R. and Sawyer, E. (2011) *Putting Analysis into Assessment: Undertaking Assessments of Need – A Toolkit for Practitioners* (2nd edn). London: National Children's Bureau.

Davies, K. and Gray, M. (2017) The place of service-user expertise in evidence-based practice. *Journal of Social Work, 17*(1), 3–20.

de Bono, E. (1985) *Six Thinking Hats: An Essential Approach to Business Management*. Boston: Little, Brown, & Company.

Department for Education (DfE) (2014) Post-qualifying standard: Knowledge and skills statement for child and family practitioners. Available at: https://assets.publishing. service.gov.uk/government/uploads/system/uploads/attachment_data/file/708704/Post-qualifying_standard-KSS_for_child_and_family_practitioners.pdf

Department for Education (DfE) (2015) Post-qualifying standard: Knowledge and skills statement for child and family practice supervisors. Available at: https://assets. publishing.service.gov.uk/government/uploads/system/uploads/attachment_data/file/708705/Post-qualifying_standard-KSS_for_child_and_family_practice_supervisors. pdf

Dewey, J. (1991) *The School and Society; and The Child and the Curriculum*. Chicago: University of Chicago Press.

Dingwall, R., Eekelaar, J. and Murray, T. (1995) *The Protection of Children: State Intervention and Family Life* (2nd edn). Aldershot: Avebury.

Dominelli, L. (2005) Social work knowledge: Contested knowledge for practice. In R. Adams, L. Dominelli and M. Payne (eds), *Social Work Futures: Crossing Boundaries, Transforming Practice* (pp. 223–236). Basingstoke: Palgrave Macmillan.

Dunne, J. (2011) Professional wisdom in practice. In L. Bondi, D. Carr, C. Clark and C. Clegg (eds), *Towards Professional Wisdom: Practical Deliberations in the People Professions* (pp. 13–26). Farnham: Ashgate.

Egan, G. (2002) *The Skilled Helper: A Problem Management and Opportunity Development Approach to Helping* (7th edn). Pacific Grove, CA: Brooks Cole.

England, H. (1986) *Social Work as Art: Making Sense for Good Practice*. London: Allen & Unwin.

Epstein, I. (2009) Promoting harmony where there is commonly conflict: Evidence-informed practice as an integrative strategy. *Social Work in Health Care, 48*, 216–231.

Fook, J. and Askeland, G. (2006) The 'critical' in critical reflection. In J. Fook, S. White and F. Gardiner (eds), *Critical Reflection in Health and Social Care*. Maidenhead: Open University Press.

Fook, J. and Askeland, G. A. (2007) Challenges of critical reflection: 'Nothing ventured, nothing gained'. *Social Work Education, 26*(5): 520–533.

Ferguson, I. (2011) *Reclaiming Social Work: Challenging Neo-liberalism and Promoting Social Justice*. London: Sage.

Gambrill, E. (2007) Critical thinking, evidence-based practice, and cognitive behavior therapy. In T. Ronen and A. Freeman (eds), *Cognitive Behavior Therapy in Clinical Social Work Practice* (pp. 67–87). New York: Springer Publishing Company.

Gibbs, G. (1988) *Learning by Doing: A Guide to Teaching and Learning Methods*. London: Further Education Unit.

Giddens, A. (1990) *The Consequences of Modernity*. Cambridge: Polity Press.

Gillett, A., Hammond, A. and Martala, M. (2009) *Successful Academic Writing*. Harlow: Pearson Education.

Giroux, H. A. (1997) *Pedagogy and the Politics of Hope: Theory, Culture, and Schooling*. Boulder, CO: Westview/HarperCollins.

Gray, M., Midgley, J. and Webb, S. (2017) *The Sage Handbook of Social Work*. London: Sage.

Gray, M., Plath, D. and Webb, S. A. (2009) *Evidence-Based Social Work: A Critical Stance*. London: Routledge.

HCPC (2017) Standards of Proficiency: Social Workers in England. Available at: https://www.hcpc-uk.org/globalassets/resources/standards/standards-of-proficiency---social-workers-in-england.pdf

Honey, P. and Mumford, A. (1982) *Manual of Learning Styles*. London: P. Honey.

Howard, L., Agnew-Davies, R. and Feder, G. (2013) *Domestic Violence and Mental Health*. London: RCPsych Publications.

Howe, D. (2008) *The Emotionally Intelligent Social Worker*. London: Macmillan International Higher Education.

International Federation of Social Workers (IFSW) (2014) *Global Standards for the Education and Training of the Social Work Profession*. Durban: IFSW.

Jansen, A. (2018) 'It's so complex!': Understanding the challenges of child protection work as experienced by newly graduated professionals. *British Journal of Social Work*, 48(6), 1524–1540.

Jiang, L. and Yang, C. (2017) User recommendation in healthcare social media by assessing user similarity in heterogeneous network. *Artificial Intelligence in Medicine*, 81, 63–77.

Jones, R. (2016) Writing skills for social workers. In K. Davies and R. Jones (eds), *Skills for Social Work Practice*. London: Palgrave.

Kiteley, R. and Stogdon, C. (2014) *Literature Reviews in Social Work*. London: Sage.

Klein, W. C. and Bloom, M. (1995) Practice wisdom. *Social Work*, 40(6), 799–807

Kolb, D. A. (1984) *Experiential Learning: Experience as the Source of Learning and Development*. Englewood Cliffs, NJ: Prentice Hall.

Kolb, D. A. and Fry, R. (1975) Toward an applied theory of experiential learning. In C. Cooper (ed.), *Theories of Group Process*. London: John Wiley.

Krumer-Nevo, M. (2016) Poverty-aware social work: A paradigm for social work practice with people in poverty. *British Journal of Social Work*, 46(6), 1793–1808.

Kübler-Ross, E. (1969) *On Death and Dying*. New York: Macmillan.

Lindsay, B. (2007) *Understanding Research and Evidence-Based Practice*. Exeter: Reflect Press.

Lishman, J. (2009) *Communication in Social Work* (2nd edn). Basingstoke: Palgrave Macmillan.

Lister, P. G. and Crisp, B. R. (2007) Critical incident analyses: A practice learning tool for students and practitioners. *Practice: Social Work in Action*, 19, 47–60.

Litchfield, M. (1999) Practice wisdom. *Advances in Nursing Science: Global Health and Nursing Practice*, 22(2), 62–73.

MacDonald, G. M. (2008) The evidence based perspective. In M. Davies (ed.), *The Blackwell Companion to Social Work* (3rd edn, pp. 434–441). Oxford: Blackwell.

Maynard, M. (1994) Methods, practice and epistemology: The debate about feminism and research. In M. Maynard and J. Purvis (eds), *Researching Women's Lives from a Feminist Perspective*. London: Taylor and Francis.

Munro, E. (2011) *The Munro Review of Child Protection: Final Report – A Child-Centred System*. London: The Stationery Office.

Osmond, J. (2005) The knowledge spectrum: A framework for teaching knowledge and its use in social work practice. *British Journal of Social Work*, 35, 881–900.

O'Sullivan, T. (2005) Some theoretical propositions on the nature of practice wisdom. *Journal of Social Work*, 5(2), 221–242.

Oxford Living Dictionary (OLD) (2018a) Definition of 'knowledge'. Available at: https://en.oxforddictionaries.com/definition/knowledge

Oxford Living Dictionary (OLD) (2018b) Defintion of 'theory'. Available at: https://en.oxforddictionaries.com/definition/theory

Parton, N. (2000) Some thoughts on the relationship between theory and practice in and for social work. *British Journal of Social Work*, 30, 449–463.

Pawson, R., Boaz, A., Grayson, L., Long, A. and Barnes, C. (2003) *Types and Quality of Knowledge in Social Care*. London: Social Care Institute for Excellence. Available at: https://www.scie.org.uk/publications/knowledgereviews/kr03.pdf

Polayni, M. (1967) *The Tacit Dimension*. London: Routledge & Kegan Paul.

Robinson, F. P. (1970) *Effective Study* (4th edn). New York: Harper & Row.

Rogers, C. (1965) *Client-centred Therapy*. Boston: Houghton Mifflin Company.

Rogers, M., Whittaker, D., Edmondson, D. and Peach, D. (2016) *Developing Skills for Social Work Practice*. London: Sage.

Rubin, A. and Bellamy, J. (2012) *Practitioner's Guide to Using Research for Evidence-Based Practice*. Hoboken, NJ: John Wiley & Sons.

Rutter, L. and Brown, K. (2015) *Critical Thinking and Professional Judgement for Social Work*. London: Learning Matters.

Saleebey, D. (2013) *The Strengths Perspective in Social Work Practice* (6th edn). Boston: Pearson.

Samson, P. L. (2015) Practice wisdom: The art and science of social work. *Journal of Social Work Practice, 29*(2), 119–131.

Schön, D. (1983) *The Reflective Practitioner: How Professionals Think In Action*. New York: Basic Books.

Sheppard, M., Newstead, S., di Caccavo, A. and Ryan, K. (2000) Reflexivity and the development of process knowledge in social work. *British Journal of Social Work, 30*(6), 863–885.

Sheridan, M. (1997) *From Birth to Five Years: Children's Developmental Progress*. London: Routledge.

Sidebotham, P., Brandon, M., Bailey, S., Belderson, P., Dodsworth, J., Garstang, J., Harrison, E., Retzer, A. and Sorensen, P. (2016) *Pathways to Harm, Pathways to Protection: A Triennial Analysis of Serious Case Reviews 2011 to 2014: Final Report*. London: Department for Education.

Smale, G. and Tuson, G., with Biehal, N. and Marsh, P. (1993) *Empowerment Assessment, Care Management and the Skilled Worker*. London: National Institute of Social Work.

Smith, R. (2009) *Doing Social Work Research*. Maidenhead: McGraw-Hill/Open University Press.

Tambe, M. and Rice, E. (2018) *Artificial Intelligence and Social Work*. Cambridge: Cambridge University Press.

The Open University (2007) *Reading and Taking Notes*. Milton Keynes: The Open University.

Thompson, N. (2010) *Theorizing Social Work Practice*. London: Palgrave Macmillan.

Trevithick, P. (2012) *Social Work Skills and Knowledge: A Practice Handbook* (3rd edn). Maidenhead: McGraw-Hill Education.

Tripp, D. (1993) *Critical Incidents in Teaching: Developing Professional Judgement*. London: Routledge.

Tuckman, B. W. (1965) Developmental sequence in small groups. *Psychological Bulletin, 63*, 384–399.

Turnell, A. and Edwards, S. (1999) *Signs of Safety: A Safety and Solution Oriented Approach to Child Protection Casework*. New York: W.W. Norton.

Turnell, A. and Essex, S. (2006) *Working with 'Denied' Child Abuse: The Resolutions Approach*. Maidenhead: Open University Press.

Veal, D., King. J. and Marston, G. (2016) Enhancing the social dimension of development: Interconnecting the capability approach and applied knowledge of social workers. *International Social Work, 61*(4), 600–612.

Webb, S. (2006) *Social Work in a Risk Society*. Basingstoke: Palgrave Macmillan.

White, S., Fook, J. and Gardner, F. (2006) *Critical Reflection in Health and Social Care*. Maidenhead: Open University Press.

Wilkins, D. and Boahen, G. (2013) *Critical Analysis Skills for Social Workers*. Maidenhead: Open University Press.

INDEX